# Trimming Yankee Sails

## Pirates and Privateers of New Brunswick

The New Brunswick Military Heritage Series, Volume 6

TRIMMING YANKEE SAILS

# Pirates and Privateers

## OF NEW BRUNSWICK

FAYE KERT

GOOSE LANE EDITIONS and
THE NEW BRUNSWICK MILITARY HERITAGE PROJECT

Edited by Marc Milner.
Cover illustrations: front: detail from *Capture of Snap Dragon*, by Irwin John Bevan (MM);
Back: *Saint John from the Signal, 1841*, by Charles Cousen (NBM).
Cover and interior design by Julie Scriver.
NBMHP cartographer: Mike Bechthold.
Printed in Canada on paper containing100% post-consumer fiber.
10 9 8 7 6 5 4 3 2

Library and Archives Canada Cataloguing in Publication

Kert, Faye
Trimming Yankee sails: pirates and privateers of
New Brunswick / Faye Kert.
(New Brunswick military heritage series; 6)
Co-published by the New Brunswick Military Heritage Project.
Includes bibliographical references and index.
ISBN 0-86492-442-9

1. Pirates — New Brunswick — History. 2. New Brunswick —
History — 1784-1867. I. New Brunswick Military Heritage Project
II. Title. III. Series.

FC2471.9.P57K47 2005 971.5'102 C2005-904697-X

Goose Lane Editions acknowledges the financial support of the Canada Council for the Arts, the Government of Canada through the Book Publishing Industry Development Program (BPIDP), and the New Brunswick Department of Wellness, Culture and Sport for its publishing activities.

Goose Lane Editions
Suite 330, 500 Beaverbrook Court
Fredericton, New Brunswick
CANADA E3B 5X4
www.gooselane.com

New Brunswick Military Heritage Project
The Brigadier Milton F. Gregg, VC,
Centre for the Study of War and Society
University of New Brunswick
PO Box 4400
Fredericton, New Brunswick
CANADA E3B 5A3
www.unb.ca/nbmhp

To all those would-be privateers, rascals and rebels —
you know who you are.

# Contents

# Trimming Yankee Sails

## Pirates and Privateers of New Brunswick

*The Bream and the Pythagoras*, by Irwin John Bevan. (MM)

# Introduction

*"I IMPLORE the Protection of the British Naval Commander, I am taken by Pirates, and have Government Stores on board, bound to Camden."*

*— Captain D. M'Waters, sloop* Mary
*1 November 1814*

On November 1, 1814, the Saint John-owned sloop *Mary* lay in Camden harbour, on the coast of Maine, where she was boarded by six armed United States revenue officers. In ordinary times this was to be expected. But by November 1814 the US and Britain had been at war for two years, and the revenue officers had come aboard from a lowly rowboat. Perhaps this was why, when the British frigate HMS *Furieuse*, Captain William Mounsey, RN, in command, hove in sight, David M'Waters, *Mary*'s master, slipped Mounsey a note complaining of his capture by "pirates" and pleading to be saved. M'Waters even offered his captors £7,000 ransom for the sloop and volunteered to stand hostage for the money. In spite of this, he was publicly accused by one of the ship's owners of signalling his Camden captors to seize the vessel so that he might also profit from their "piracy."

It appears that *Mary* had indeed been captured by Americans after all: in the court process that followed, M'Waters was proven innocent by the sworn statements of the his captors, *Mary*'s officers, passengers and crew. His worse offence seems to have been that he mistook Camden for Castine, where he was bound with supplies for the British occupying force. But M'Waters still had to publish his denials in the local Saint

John papers to clear his name. The accusation that he had conspired to have his ship and cargo captured was a crude attempt by one of the sloop's owners, Gabriel Fowler, to force M'Waters to pay for the owners' loss. The character assassination, court testimony and newspaper stories involved M'Waters and *Mary*'s owners, Fowler and Benjamin Darling of Saint John, New Brunswick, in a lengthy wrangle that outlasted the War of 1812.

The fact that M'Waters had to work so hard to clear his name speaks volumes for the acceptance of such collusion between apparent enemies and the grey legal area of capture at sea. Indeed, as in all areas where international borders cut across economic and social interests, piracy, privateering, smuggling and arranged capture were all employed by entrepreneurial New Brunswickers in the nineteenth century. The Bay of Fundy, the Gulf of Maine and the waters of the western Atlantic were all part of a tightly interconnected seafaring community. When formal war, like the War of 1812, interrupted those familiar trading and social patterns, people on both sides adapted and situations at sea were not always what they seemed. American ships took out licences to continue trade with the British Empire, which was very much in need of American grain. Small traders flew false flags in order to deceive naval patrols and privateers, or — if they were privateering vessels — to trick an intended prize. And, in some cases, as was alleged with the sloop *Mary* in November 1814, capture could be arranged with friends in the other country so the prize and her cargo could be bought back cheap at auction inside the enemy blockade and the goods then resold by a local agent for a handsome profit for everyone. Mistaken identity, collaborating with the enemy, false colours, phony captures, smuggling, blockade running and profitable prize making were all part of New Brunswick's daring and devious nineteenth-century maritime history.

Private war at sea was a feature of every naval war and colonial conflict from the late medieval period until it was banned by international agreement in 1856 — at least by every developed nation except the United States: they continued the practice until after their Civil War in the 1860s. The waging of private war at sea developed in an era when kings did not have navies in the modern sense and there were few means for either attacking an enemy at sea during war or recouping commercial losses due to enemy action. Since traders owned fleets of ships armed for protection against pirates, it was a simple matter for the King to issue his subjects with "Letters of Marque and Reprisal," making them "privateers." These commissions granted civilians the legal right to both wage war on the enemy and, in the process, to recover their own costs — or commercial losses to enemy war vessels. A very fine line separated pirates from privateers, but that line, often no thicker than the paper on which a letter of marque was written, entitled the privateer to wage war on the enemy of his state and to keep most of the proceeds from the vessels he captured, his "prizes." A pirate doing the same thing without a licence would be hanged.

Privateers were also obliged to follow strict rules for disposing of their captures: they had to be taken to a port that had a Vice-Admiralty Court, and the legality of the capture had to be proven before a judge. Once the judge ruled that the prize was "good and lawful," the ship and/or cargo would be sold at auction and the proceeds shared among owners, officers and crew according to their pre-cruise agreement. Since Royal Navy vessels were also entitled to prize money and naval officers counted on prizes to supplement their salaries, public and private armed vessels frequently found themselves competing for captures.

Because seaborne trade was the lifeblood of commercial nations, privateering or commerce raiding was also an effective way of draining the enemy's will to fight by emptying his wallet. But it wasn't easy. Storms, shoals, combat and capture lurked along every coast, and many a successful capture evaporated when the hard-won prize was recaptured by the enemy, sank after battle or was overturned in court. In spite of — or maybe because of — the danger, privateering attracted young, adventurous men who were keen to fight for king and country — if the price was right. While most of them behaved like respectable law-abiding citizens, even those who did not tried to limit the risks to their property, their prizes and their lives.

New Brunswick's earliest European settlers, such as Charles de St. Etienne de La Tour, who was granted the seigneury along the lower St. John River in the early seventeenth century, engaged in the practice of private war at sea. During the Acadia Civil War of the 1640s, La Tour and his arch-rival, Charles de Menou d'Aulnay at Port Royal across the Bay of Fundy, pillaged and sacked each other's establishments and ships. Both drew their legitimacy for such actions from their conflicting claims to a royal commission from the King of France: to have done otherwise would have made them both pirates.

New Brunswick was too thinly settled through the seventeenth and eighteenth centuries to consistently produce notable participants in the many naval wars of the era. That did not stop New Englanders and the Dutch from raiding and burning Acadian settlements, nor privateers from Maine from plundering the coastline during the American Revolution. The latter included snatching the brig *Loyal Briton* from under the guns of Fort Frederick in Saint John harbour in 1776, then capturing the "garrison" of a corporal and two privates. By the time the American pirate-turned-privateer Agreen Crabtree returned to Saint John the next year, Fort Howe had been built and substantial guns installed. After that privateers never raided the port city again.

The settlement of the Loyalists in southern New Brunswick after the American Revolution finally provided the commercial foundations needed to support private war at sea. As a rule, a privateering campaign needed ships, men and capital in order to function, and it was not until the early decades of the nineteenth century that Saint John possessed these necessary ingredients on a sufficient scale. Typically, businessmen already engaged in trading either found their regular commerce so disrupted by war that they hoped to maintain a cash flow by plundering the trade of their erstwhile friends, or they armed their regular trading vessels, secured letters of marque and then captured whatever enemy vessel they cared to try their luck against. The declaration of war against the

United States in 1812 was, therefore, the first and only time in which New Brunswick actively participated in privateering.

Such warfare was already of dubious value and legality, but many New Brunswickers quietly operated according to their own rules as well. Smugglers disguised themselves as fishermen, and occasionally privateer "captures" were pre-arranged with business colleagues from "enemy" ports. If David M'Waters couldn't tell a Customs official from a pirate, it is easy to see why privateers, especially the less well-behaved ones, were often mistaken for their piratical brothers.

Although privateering was outlawed by international agreement in the Treaty of Paris of 1856, the complex and entrepreneurial nature of private war against the enemy did not stop there. The United States refused to sign the Treaty of Paris, and so when their Civil War began in 1861, both the Union and Confederate governments issued letters of marque and reprisal. This left an opening for an enterprising Southerner and a gang of largely New Brunswick ne'er-do-wells to engage in one of North America's last acts of private war — or piracy: the capture of the SS *Chesapeake*. The event has all the hallmarks of a comic opera or a Hollywood film, and it exposed the grey areas of maritime law. It also revealed where Maritimers' sympathies lay and indicated that, well into the nineteenth century, Atlantic Canadians were not averse to trimming Yankee sails when they could get the chance — on the sea or in the courtroom.

"*Boats from HMS Maidstone Capture the Commodore Barry*," by Irwin John Bevan, 1852-1940. A month after her capture in August 1812, the *Commodore Barry* was purchased by the New Brunswick government, commissioned as *Brunswicker*, and sent off to defend shipping in the Bay of Fundy. (MM)

## Chapter One

# New Brunswick's Undeclared War, 1812

In June 1812, the United States of America declared war on Great Britain. But New Brunswickers and their neighbours to the south were not suddenly formal enemies. In fact, the last thing the British Empire — by 1812 at war with France off and on for nearly twenty years — needed was another war. With the exception of Spain, where Britain's small army was waging a successful resistance lead by the Duke of Wellington, and Russia, all of Europe was under Napoleon's yoke. Only the world beyond Europe lay outside Napoleon's grasp, and access to that world and its trade was effectively controlled by the Royal Navy. Indeed, it was the sheer weight of British seapower, and its control over the free movement of people and trade, that ultimately drove America to its declaration of war. And it was the British desire to avoid that conflict by not immediately declaring war in response that left New Brunswick uniquely vulnerable in the summer and fall of 1812. The results were the waging of a four-month undeclared war by Lieutenant-Governor Smyth and the first and only privateering campaign launched by New Brunswick in the great age of sail.

War with the United States offered New Brunswick merchants, shipowners and seamen three options: licensed trading, licensed warfare or smuggling. While hundreds of licences were issued to ensure a steady supply of flour and other foodstuffs to British soldiers, sailors and colonial subjects — including New Brunswick — at least ten New Brunswick-owned vessels also received one or more letters of marque entitling them to seize American shipping. The fact that many of these vessels do not appear to have made any prizes suggests that either privateering was not their primary focus or some may have used their letters of marque to disguise more covert activities. The majority of individuals and companies who participated in this activity were based in Saint John, but merchants and entrepreneurs from St. Andrews and Fredericton were also represented among the more than twenty individuals and businesses who invested in privateering between 1812 and 1814.

It is ironic that although New Brunswick was part of the most powerful maritime empire the world has ever seen, there was virtually nothing available in the summer of 1812 to protect its coasts from American depredations. Nearly two decades of war with France had reduced Britain's thousand-ship navy that had triumphed at Trafalgar to a thin wooden line. The Royal Navy was so stretched just trying to protect its merchant trade from attacks by French and Spanish enemies in Europe and the West Indies, it could only spare twenty-seven vessels for the whole North American station that stretched from Newfoundland to the Caribbean. Many of these vessels were small, old or unseaworthy, and almost all of them spent from November to July protecting British shipping in and out of Bermuda.

The United States Navy was not much better prepared for war in early 1812. With no ships-of-the-line, seven frigates (a few dating back to the Revolution), and some smaller vessels, no dockyards and no real plan of action, the US Navy was undermanned, under-gunned and overwhelmed. Former President Thomas Jefferson had allowed the small American navy built up during the Revolution and the quasi-war with France in the 1790s to rot at the dock. The only solution for the United States was privateering. Two Baltimore schooners, the *Nonsuch* and the *Rossie*, shared the honour of privateering commission number one. Within days, dozens of captains and ship owners from Baltimore, New York and Salem were besieging their state governors for letters of marque.

Exposed and vulnerable to attack in its home waters, Atlantic Canada's self-reliant maritime community took similar steps to protect itself even before Britain's declaration of war in October. By 1812, most New

MacPherson's Tavern (also known as the Exchange Coffee House), Scotch Row, Saint John, ca. 1812. Much of the business of privateering was arranged in such places, sometimes even the Vice-Admiralty Prize Court, and MacPherson's Tavern was probably no exception. ( NAC C-073563)

Brunswick sailors, fishermen, merchants and ship owners knew the rules and regulations governing privateering. A formal declaration of war was usually followed by a prize act that allowed the government to issue letters of marque, or commissions, that entitled the holder to seize enemy vessels as prizes. To confirm that the vessel and cargo really were enemy property, that the capture had been legal, and that the crew and cargo properly treated, the captor was obliged to send the prize into port, where it was adjudicated by an Admiralty Court judge. In British North America, Lieutenant-Governors John Coape Sherbrooke of Nova Scotia and George Stracey Smyth of New Brunswick were responsible for issuing letters of marque, and the Vice-Admiralty Court in Halifax monitored legal matters.

Once a prize was "condemned" or awarded to the captor and the vessel and/or cargo auctioned off, investors, officers and crews received their agreed-upon shares reasonably quickly. Despite court costs, salvage fees, the repayment of the costs of arming and equipping the privateer itself and other charges related to securing a prize, and provided risks to life and property were kept to a minimum, profits could be substantial. The New Brunswick privateer *Dart* is said to have earned each of her crew roughly $500 from their first cruise, a considerable amount given the average seaman of the period earned $15 to $30 per month. Although some considered privateering no more than legalized piracy, North America's maritime communities welcomed privateering as a respectable, legitimate, effective and often profitable way of waging war.

The US declaration of war was signed on June 18, 1812, but communication was so poor at the time that news of the war did not reach Halifax for over a week. The news finally arrived on June 27, when the frigate HMS *Belvidera* (36 guns) limped into port with several dead and wounded sailors aboard. Three days earlier off Nantucket, Captain Byron, RN, had learned about the war the hard way — fighting off a determined attack by two 44-gun US Navy frigates, USS *President* and *Constitution,* and three smaller vessels under Commodore Rodgers. Surprised and seriously outgunned, Byron narrowly managed to escape the engagement but did seize three American vessels on his way home just to get even. The same day, a despatch boat from St. Andrews carried the news to the inhabitants of Saint John. Ready or not, on July 30 Captain Broke of HMS *Shannon* — later famous for its successful action against the USS *Chesapeake* off Boston — smugly declared that the British North American squadron "is in excellent service order and confident of destroying our Enemy's little Navy if we are fortunate enough to meet them."

Not everyone in the US, as we shall see, was pleased about the prospect of war with Britain, but President Madison, the Republicans and many along the mid-Atlantic seaboard were ready to fight. Emotions ran high. On June 20, 1812, Baltimore's *Federal Republican* newspaper dared to criticize the government for rushing into war unprepared, and the next day a mob set its offices on fire. Soon the American coast was bristling with privateers ranging from heavily armed ships of several hundred tons carrying more than 150 men to open whaleboats manned by a few men

*The Capture of the British Merchantman Quebec by the American Privateer Saratoga*, artist unknown. *Saratoga* was typical of the small, fast Baltimore Clipper-type ships that dominated privateering in the War of 1812. *Quebec* yielded a staggering $300,000 in prize money. (NAC C-040581)

armed with muskets. Some were so small that, in one case, the privateer was carried home on the deck of her prize! Ironically known as "shaving mills," these small open boats, mostly from the coast of Maine, were rowed by up to thirty or so scruffy-looking men with little regard for either shaving or the finer rules of private armed warfare, especially those that prohibited attacks on land. Vessels such as the *Weazel* of Castine, terrorized inhabitants along the Fundy coast with frequent raids on shore and thefts of food, fishing gear and even women's clothing.

The Royal Navy's early attempts to sweep these small privateers from the Bay of Fundy drew blood on both sides. In early August 1812, in a harbour near Quoddy, Maine, HMS *Maidstone* and *Spartan*, 36 and 38 guns respectively, tried to seize the Portland privateers *Mars* and *Morningstar* mounting a couple of small guns each. Having been warned of the attack, the privateers fought back fiercely, killing or wounding twenty men before being forced to lower their flag. Respectful of the tenacity of their opponents, the British later sent ten boats and two hundred men to remove the captured crews and burn the vessels. A few days later, HMs hips *Indian, Plumper*, *Spartan* and *Maidstone* cautiously sent five barges and 250 men to attack the US Revenue Cutter *Commodore Barry* and the privateers *Madison*, *Olive* and *Spruce* carrying probably less than fifty crew altogether. During the first few months of undeclared war, Royal Navy vessels succeeded in capturing the US naval brig *Nautilus*, thirteen privateers, a revenue cutter, fifteen ships, four brigs, ten schooners and a sloop. On the other hand, with the exception of a few prizes taken by the USS *Essex*, most of the early American prizes were sent in by privateers.

President Madison's declaration of war also caused great anxiety among the inhabitants of the District of Maine, who shared a long history and longer border with New Brunswick. In Saint John, readers of the *Royal Gazette and Saint John Advertiser* opened their papers on June 27 to read the following:

> WAR! WAR! WAR! . . . The Inhabitants of East Port held a meeting this morning, when it was unanimously agreed to preserve a good understanding with the Inhabitants of New-Brunswick, and to discountenance all depredations on the property of each other. We also learn, that the Embodied Militia were ordered out.

During the long years of war against Napoleon, New England shipping interests had lost hundreds of ships, cargoes and crews to France and her Spanish, Neapolitan and Dutch allies. Along with the direct loss of property it caused, war at sea dramatically reduced trading opportunities and increased risk of capture by naval vessels and privateers. This raised insurance rates and drove up wages and shipping costs. The merchants knew all too well that the cost of this new war would likely come out of their pockets. Moreover, the economies of Maine and New Brunswick were closely linked, while the British depended heavily on American trade — especially agricultural products and the white pine cut in the forests of northern Maine and in the disputed territory of the upper St. John River.

## *The Licensed Trade*

To secure the good will of Americans, Admiral Herbert Sawyer, commander of naval forces in North America, ordered his naval captains to treat any prisoners of war from the New England states with "great indulgence" and urged his men to avoid capturing small vessels of no value. By offering economic incentives to the merchants in nearby Maine, he hoped they would be less likely to turn to privateering and help to secure their continued trade with the British Empire. First, Sawyer convinced the Nova Scotia Executive Council to admit American goods traded duty-free at Eastport on Moose Island, Maine. Then British military, naval and civilian authorities began to issue licences to American ships willing to carry flour and provisions to feed British troops fighting Napoleon in Spain and Portugal.

Since New Brunswick could barely grow enough to feed its own population of seven thousand let alone extra British forces, it was critical that the existing trade between Maine and New Brunswick continue. Not only did St. Andrews' citizens depend almost entirely on their American neighbours for flour, but the market at Saint John relied heavily on American oats and hay. In return for foodstuffs and a variety of contraband articles, New Brunswickers happily traded lumber, fish and cash. Neither side allowed a little thing like a declaration of war to interfere with their longstanding, usually legal, commercial activities.

During the first two and a half months of undeclared war, some five hundred licenses issued to Americans insured a steady supply of flour and provisions to British North America and the West Indies, to British troops in Europe and to British fleets in American waters. As early as July 15, the Commissariat in Saint John was advertising for fresh beef for His Majesty's ships, and many of those who responded were Americans. At a time when money was scarce and British forces were offering hard cash, practical Yankee farmers felt that if the Royal Navy was buying beef it might as well be American. And how could a farmer be blamed if his cattle just happened to graze near the border where New Brunswickers could entice the animals across with baskets of corn? While some Americans balked at supplying enemy troops in North America, both the US Treasury Department and the US Attorney General's office ruled that licensed trade with British troops in Spain was not illegal. Whether it was moral or not was up to the individual conscience of the supplier.

Despite British attempts to keep Americans from slipping into privateering, the war descended on the New Brunswick coast almost immediately. On June 30, 1812, an extraordinary issue of the *Royal Gazette and Saint John Advertiser* reprinted the American declaration of war. Two days later, Nova Scotia's Lieutenant-Governor Sherbrooke issued a proclamation urging residents of New Brunswick and Nova Scotia to "abstain from molesting the inhabitants living on the shores of the United States" as long as the Americans left them alone. The Baltimore *Niles Weekly Register* denounced Sherbrooke's proclamation as an attempt to encourage treason, but he had little choice. Scrambling to end the conflict by diplomacy rather than combat, the British government refused to issue a declaration of war right away. It was not until October 13, 1812, nearly four months after the American declaration, that Britain officially declared war.

In the meantime, Sherbrooke and Smyth in New Brunswick were caught in a legal no man's land. Without a declaration of war there could be no letters of marque and no privateers, yet something clearly had to be done to respond to the undeclared war in the Bay of Fundy and Gulf of Maine. Moreover, provincial merchants and ship owners, afraid that the navy would capture all the prizes before they could get to sea, clamoured for commissions to protect themselves and their property. Sherbrooke's solution to the tricky problem of undeclared war was to issue carefully worded letters of marque under his own authority. His first letter, issued against France and the Batavian Republic [the Netherlands], provided the large 623-ton armed trader *Caledonia* with the option of prize making on a transatlantic voyage in July 1812. In August, Sherbrooke issued a second letter of marque against France and unspecified "other enemies of the King of England" to the famous schooner *Liverpool Packet*, Atlantic Canada's most successful privateer. A former slave ship turned packet vessel then privateer, the *Liverpool Packet* brought at least fifty prizes into court and destroyed or released many more. Her numerous cruises under several captains, among them Caleb Seeley of New Brunswick, earned her a reputation as the evil genius of the American coasting trade and enriched her owners with thousands of dollars in prize money. Since New Brunswick's maritime settlements were under a similar threat, Lieutenant-Governor Smyth had no choice but to follow suit: in the summer and late fall of 1812 New Brunswick fought back.

## *Provincial Privateer Chasers*

In early July, the *Nova Scotia Gazette* noted that the 21-ton privateer sloop *Jefferson* of Salem, Massachusetts, had gone ashore at Moose Island, home to both British and American citizens. Despite a warning from the local American Committee of Safety not to harm any of the inhabitants, the privateer sailed into Snug Cove and boldly cut the mooring cable of a British schooner. Fortunately for her owners, the vessel drifted ashore and escaped capture. This scare might have prompted a later report that some inhabitants of Moose Island who were removing their families and estates to the mainland had been insulted and threatened by American privateers.

While residents of New Brunswick and their neighbours in Maine generally agreed to live and let live, infrequent acts of hostility kept both sides on edge. On July 9, the fiery British owner of Campobello Island, David Owen, was attacked in his own bedroom by two Eastport men who threatened to kill him and burn down his house. A month later, in the Saint John *Royal Gazette*, the outraged Owen offered "400 Dollars Reward" for the capture of John Stedman Beckwith and his accomplice, Thorndyke, who "did with violence seize me by the throat, with blows upon my head, and wounding of my right eye." Fortunately, Beckwith's "want of superior strength" and the arrival of Owen's staff prevented worse harm, but the two men only managed to escape being killed by Owen's "lenity and forbearance." A month later, Owen appeared determined to track them down.

Such fears were part of the almost-daily reports of privateer sightings at the mouth of the Bay of Fundy and off Mount Desert. In response to a rumour that American privateers intended to cut out a large ship loading at Digdegush, New Brunswick, some thirty or forty volunteers from St. Andrews rushed to assist the ship, although the attack never came. On August 3, the *Portland Gazette*, reported that a privateer crew had gone to Grand Manan, New Brunswick, and boarded a vessel that had been hauled up and stripped of sails. They ransacked nearby houses and wharves and threatened the unarmed inhabitants with death unless the sails were produced. Eventually they found part of the sails and made off with the vessel, worth, perhaps, $50. The writer concluded "If our government allows of *land privateering*, they ought to send us a sufficient forcc to ward off the blow, should the English retaliate." The Royal Navy's response to these depredations along the New Brunswick shoreline was to assign the small, 4-gun, 80-ton naval schooner HMS *Bream* to Saint John. She was tasked with patrolling the entire Bay of Fundy.

Clearly this was not enough, and in early September 1812, Lieutenant-Governor George Smyth was forced to act. He purchased, as a prize recently condemned in Halifax after her capture in August, the former US Revenue Cutter *Commodore Barry* on behalf of the province and renamed the sloop *Brunswicker.* The current Naval Reserve Division in Saint John, HMCS *Brunswicker*, perpetuates the name. A privateer-chaser rather than a naval vessel or a privateer, *Brunswicker* was part of Smyth's strategy to reassure New Brunswick's shipping interests. On September 19, 1812, Smyth issued a letter of marque for the small 39-ton 4-gun sloop. Under this commission, *Brunswicker* was ordered to protect the province from His Majesty's enemies, particularly the United States, and to reinforce HMS *Bream*. According to her letter of marque, *Brunswicker* was to observe all of His Majesty's instructions for commanders of naval vessels of war and privateers, observe the directions issued in a proclamation of July 10, 1812, and leave alone any unarmed American vessels licensed to bring provisions or other non-military goods into Nova Scotia. Lastly, *Brunswicker* was expected to lend aid to any of His Majesty's ships and vessels of war when required. It did not take long for her to ship a crew of twenty-five eager New Brunswick volunteers. Although he was later reprimanded by the British Foreign Office for issuing a commission before the official declaration of war, Smyth felt his actions were justified.

Under captains James Read and later Joseph Rideout, *Brunswicker* carried out numerous patrols in company with HMS *Bream*. Newspapers in both New Brunswick and the United States eagerly noted the comings and goings of each other's privateers. When the Saint John *Royal Gazette* mentioned that *Bream* and *Brunswicker* were chasing two American privateers reported off Point Lepreau in late November (by which time Britain had declared war), some twenty men off different ships in Saint John harbour offered to join the hunt. Boston's *Columbian Centinel* later told its readers that the privateers *Fame* and *Revenge* of Salem and *Industry* of Lynn had been chased out of the Bay of Fundy on November 23 by *Bream* and the sloop "New Brunswick," and that their fate was unknown. In fact, the *Revenge* was captured on December 4 by HMS *La Paz* and went on to become the Nova Scotia privateer *Retaliation*.

*Brunswicker* also supported the navy in other ways. In December 1812, HMS *Plumper* was lost in a storm in the Bay of Fundy along with her captain, Lieutenant Hare, two midshipmen and thirty-eight crewmen. As the *Royal Gazette* sadly reported, only the pilot, a midshipman and twenty-eight men got safely to shore. Since she had been carrying £20,000 in coin, *Brunswicker* and *Bream* were watching the wreck and had helped retrieve £5,000 of it. *Brunswicker* was effective but expensive. In January, Smyth asked the provincial council for an extra twenty men to serve aboard *Brunswicker* at a cost of about £500 for four months. If no support were forthcoming, he would have to discharge the vessel. Despite some skepticism by members of council, Smyth must have received his funding because there are reports of *Brunswicker* off Passamaquoddy Bay in early March 1813 and in Saint John at the end of the month. After that, *Brunswicker* seems to have been retired.

As a companion or perhaps a successor to *Brunswicker*, Smyth commissioned a second privateer-chaser in December 1812. On loan from the Superintendent of Trade and Fisheries, the armed schooner *Hunter* was employed to escort trading vessels through the gauntlet of American privateers hovering around the Bay of Fundy and the Nova Scotia coast. On Christmas Eve, she arrived in Halifax with a brig from Saint John and on December 30, citing "Intelligence from Eastport," the *Boston Patriot* reported her back at Saint John with a convoy from Halifax. With no prizes to her credit and no further references after 1812, *Hunter* also seems to have either been retired or returned to her original duties.

## *Licensed Warfare*

Clearly a handful of provincial and naval vessels could not protect the entire Atlantic coast in the early months of the war, and despite the fact that communities like Eastport, Maine, prided themselves on never launching a privateer, there were plenty of other Yankees eager to risk their lives for a share in the prize money. During the first six months of war, shipping news from Boston, New York, Halifax and Saint John recorded dozens of ships sailing to and from New Brunswick that were stopped, seized or burnt by American privateers. Royal Navy ships recaptured at least half of them and a further three were retaken by New Brunswick's first real privateer, the aptly named *General Smyth*.

At 48 tons, the single-masted sloop *General Smyth* boasted four guns and a crew of sixty, and eventually represented a very heavy investment by the businessmen of Saint John. On July 28, 1812, Joseph Rideout, one of her owners and one of *Brunswicker's* later captains, agreed to sell a half share to merchants William and Munson Jarvis for £50. In return for their paying one-twentieth of the costs of the privateer on its first and future cruises, the brothers would be entitled to receive one-twentieth of the profits. The list of more than a dozen owners and investors in the *General Smyth* reads like a who's who of the Saint John commercial establishment. They include her first captain, George Raymond, as well as merchants David Merritt, Daniel Lovett, James Thorpe Hanford, George Leonard Jr., William Donaldson, Benjamin Stanton, Felix Thomas, Samuel Nichols and Robert Shives.

On her first cruise, the *General Smyth* seized two prizes, one British and one American. The brig *Penelope,* of St. John's, Newfoundland, loaded with a valuable cargo of rum, sugar, coffee and molasses was recaptured in mid-August from the American privateer *Orlando*, while the Machias, Maine, schooner *Fortune*, with a cargo of boards and rum, was taken a couple of weeks later. Since *Penelope* and most of her cargo were owned by British subjects, she was returned to her owners. The remaining cargo — thirteen casks of coffee — was part of a two-year legal battle that cost the owners hundreds of pounds in court fees. As for the *General Smyth*, since both ships were seized before the official declaration of war, the prizes were condemned to the Crown rather than the captors thus depriving the privateers of their anticipated prize money.

*General Smyth*'s next cruise under Captain Joseph Rideout was somewhat more successful, although her first prize, *Reward*, taken October 10 turned out to have a licence from Admiral Sawyer entitling her to carry her cargo of flour, peas, potatoes and dried fish from Salem, Massachusetts, to Lisbon for Wellington's army. The Vice-Admiralty Court, apparently ignoring the licence, awarded the *Reward* to the Crown because Britain had still not declared war on the United States. Because of the substantial value of the cargo, assessed at £5,536.12.2, the owners appealed the decision. Six months later and considerably worse for wear, the *Reward* and its remaining cargo were restored to the owner — but only after he paid £693 in court costs. *General Smyth's* crew and their investors got nothing. It was not until late October, after the British declaration of war, that *General Smyth's* crew finally took a prize they were allowed to keep. The 90-ton schooner *Lydia* was on her way to Baltimore with a cargo of fish and lumber when she was carried into Saint John. Although claimed by the court, the *Lydia* and her cargo, appraised at £889.17.6 were eventually condemned as lawful prize.

Described in the *Boston Patriot* of October 17, 1812, as one of several "non-descript annoying machines" bothering American trade, the *General Smyth* does not seem to have taken any more prizes that year. Evidence that the privateer was out cruising in 1813 comes from an account of the

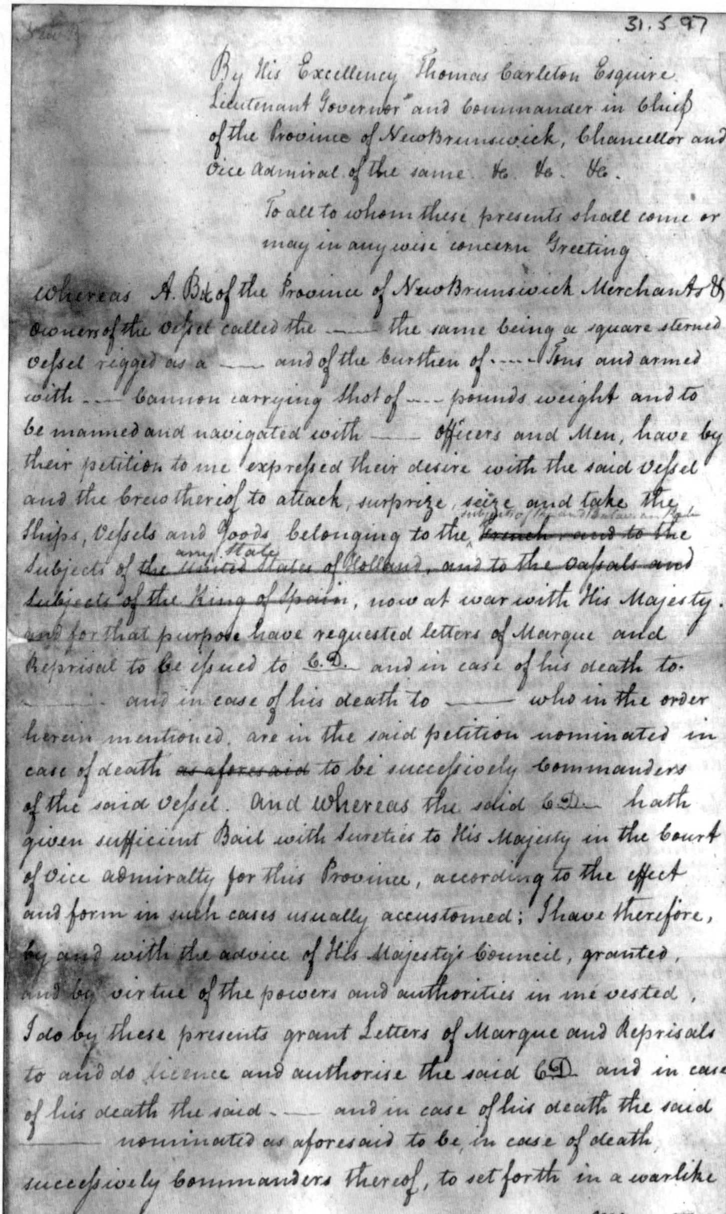

31.5 97

By His Excellency Thomas Carleton Esquire Lieutenant Governor and Commander in Chief of the Province of New Brunswick, Chancellor and Vice Admiral of the same &c. &c. &c.

To all to whom these presents shall come or may in anywise concern Greeting

Whereas A. B. of the Province of New Brunswick Merchants & Owners of the Vessel called the —— the same being a square sterned Vessel rigged as a —— and of the burthen of —— Tons and armed with —— Cannon carrying shot of —— pounds weight and to be manned and navigated with —— Officers and Men, have by their petition to me expressed their desire with the said Vessel and the Crew thereof to attack, surprize, seize and take the Ships, Vessels and Goods belonging to the ~~French and to the~~ Subjects of ~~the United States of Holland, and to the Vassals and Subjects of the King of Spain~~, now at war with His Majesty. ~~and~~ for that purpose have requested letters of Marque and Reprisal to be issued to C.D. and in case of his death to —— and in case of his death to —— who in the order herein mentioned, are in the said petition nominated in case of death ~~as aforesaid~~ to be successively Commanders of the said Vessel. And Whereas the said C.D. hath given sufficient Bail with Sureties to His Majesty in the Court of Vice Admiralty for this Province, according to the effect and form in such cases usually accustomed; I have therefore, by and with the advice of His Majesty's Council, granted, and by virtue of the powers and authorities in me vested, I do by these presents grant Letters of Marque and Reprisals to and do licence and authorise the said C.D. and in case of his death the said —— and in case of his death the said —— nominated as aforesaid to be, in case of death, successively Commanders thereof, to set forth in a warlike manner.

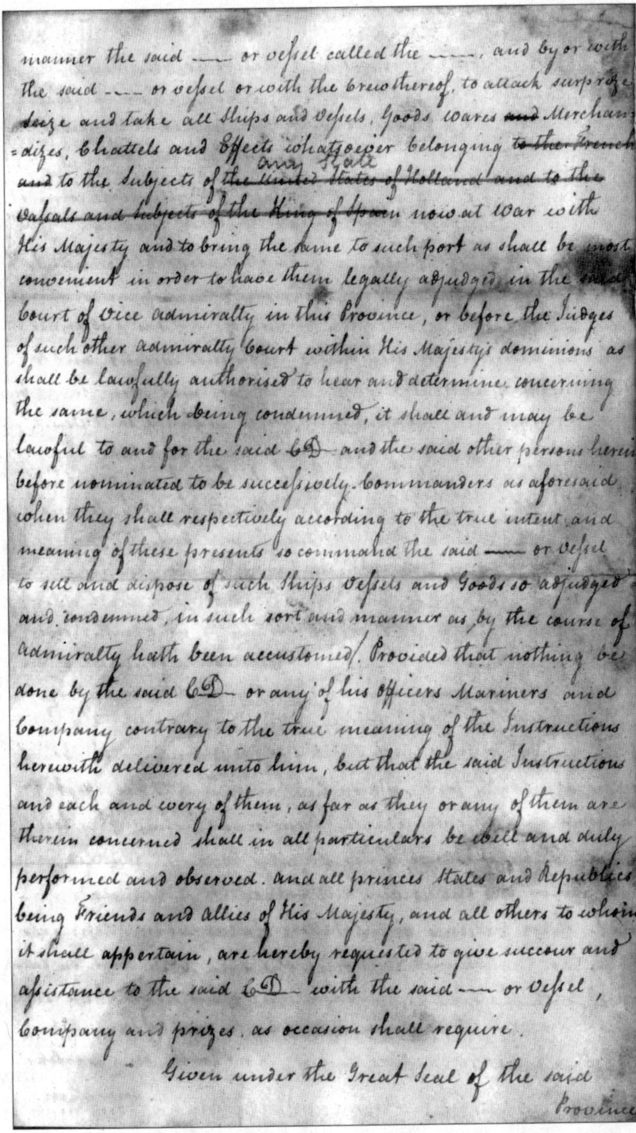
manner the said —— or Vessel called the ——, and by or with the said —— or Vessel or with the Crew thereof, to attack surprize seize and take all Ships and Vessels, Goods Wares ~~and~~ Merchan=dizes, Chattels and Effects whatsoever belonging ~~to the French and~~ to the Subjects of any State ~~the United States of Holland and to the Vassals and Subjects of the King of Spain~~ now at War with His Majesty and to bring the same to such port as shall be most convenient in order to have them legally adjudged in the said Court of Vice admiralty in this Province, or before the Judges of such other admiralty Court within His Majesty's dominions as shall be lawfully authorised to hear and determine concerning the same, which being condemned, it shall and may be lawful to and for the said C.D. and the said other persons herein before nominated to be successively Commanders as aforesaid when they shall respectively according to the true intent and meaning of these presents so command the said —— or Vessel to sell and dispose of such Ships Vessels and Goods so adjudged and condemned, in such sort and manner as by the course of admiralty hath been accustomed/. Provided that nothing be done by the said C.D. or any of his Officers Mariners and Company contrary to the true meaning of the Instructions herewith delivered unto him, but that the said Instructions and each and every of them, as far as they or any of them are therein concerned shall in all particulars be well and duly performed and observed. and all princes States and Republics being Friends and Allies of His Majesty, and all others to whom it shall appertain, are hereby requested to give succour and assistance to the said C.D. with the said —— or Vessel, Company and prizes as occasion shall require.

Given under the Great Seal of the said Province

Application for a Letter of Marque submitted to Lieutenant-Governor George Stracey Smyth by a group of Saint John merchants in July, 1812. The privateer ended up being the *General Smyth*. (PANB) daring escape of one of her prizes in the *Boston Patriot* of August 7 that year. A week earlier, the sloop *Reliance* (Captain Hancock) sailed from St. George's River for Boston. She had just left port in company with five coasting vessels when she was taken by a privateer sloop referred to as "General Smith." A prize master was put on board and the sloop ordered back to New Brunswick. Soon after, however, the American privateer *Siro*, from Portland, hove into sight. Anxious to keep out of her way, the *General Smyth* and her four prizes moved "to the Eastward." As *Reliance* fell farther behind, Captain Hancock wrested the sword from the prize master, secured him, and brought the *Reliance* into Portland five hours later. According to the article, the prize crew for *Reliance* was not fully manned because the privateer had no men to spare, having sent them all off in prizes and intending to convoy whatever vessels she captured home. That miscalculation may well have marked the end of *General Smyth*'s privateering career.

*General Smyth* was not the only New Brunswick letter of marque ship to operate during 1812. It appears that the 14-gun sloop *Comet* under Captain John Eddington was engaged in escort duty during the undeclared war. Although her commission has not been found, the Saint John *Royal Gazette* of September 14, 1812, published a segment of *Comet*'s log from September 10 to September 11 describing an attack by the American privateer *Teazer* of New York, identifiable by her blue pennant with a white T on it. According to the *Comet*'s log, she and her companion, the ship *Ned* (or *Naiad*) from Glasgow (Captain Nicol) were in the Bay of Fundy en route for Saint John when an unidentified ship approached them flying one too many English flags. Suspicious, both Eddington and Nicol exchanged shots with the vessel before it finally ran up the American flag and threatened to board the *Ned*. Eddington "gave him our seven larboard guns, which made him heave about, and prevented him from boarding." After a brief chase, *Comet* watched *Teazer* haul down her colours and "set all sail before the wind." In return for helping Nicol to escape the *Teazer*'s clutches, Eddington received two barrels of gunpowder and returned safely to Saint John.

A few weeks later her Saint John owners, Messrs. John Black and Company, advertised "generous wages" for twenty able-bodied seamen and landsmen to complete *Comet*'s crew for her next cruise under Captain Eddington. No more is heard of *Comet*, leaving one wondering whether she continued to sail as a letter of marque or was eventually captured.

As for *Ned*, the ship's fate unfolds in the journal of the Salem privateer *Revenge,* reprinted in the Saint John *Royal Gazette,* November 30,1812. Slowly making her way from Saint John to Glasgow with a full cargo of timber, the 400-ton copper-bottomed *Ned* was a tempting prize. *Revenge*, a small 57-ton schooner armed with one long gun and two small 3-pounders, caught sight of her off Grand Manan and chased her for five hours. Once she was close enough to engage, *Revenge* hoisted her colours and fired her large gun but to little effect against such a large target. Undaunted, the privateer hauled alongside *Ned* and "kept up a brisk fire with our large gun and muskets, during which time she gave us her whole broadside." After three and a half hours of constant firing back and forth, the rigging and sails of both vessels were cut to shreds and the privateer was nearly out of ammunition. But by then, the sixteen men aboard *Ned* had clearly had enough. When a dozen privateersmen armed with pistols and swords prepared to board her, "she struck her colors." Amazingly, despite the prolonged engagement, only *Ned*'s mate and carpenter were slightly wounded and just one of the privateers suffered an injured leg.

Having boldly captured a plump prize practically on New Brunswick's doorstep, Captain John Sinclair Jr. was not destined to enjoy it. On December 4, *Revenge* fell in with HMS *La Paz* and was sent in to Halifax still carrying fourteen English prisoners on board from two earlier prizes. The privateer was duly condemned to her captors in the Vice-Admiralty Court, and on January 29, 1813, she was purchased for £530 by Snow Parker and Thomas Freeman of Liverpool, Nova Scotia. Repaired and re-armed with five guns and fifty men, she sailed out of Liverpool on the first of three successful cruises as the fittingly-named Nova Scotia privateer *Retaliation*.

## *Smuggling*

Privateering and licensed trade provided New Brunswickers with two legal options for continuing commercial activity in time of war, but there was also a third option: the time-honoured tradition of smuggling. Indeed, given the ragged coastline of both Maine and New Brunswick, the labyrinth of islands in the Passamaquoddy Bay, and the family and economic ties that straddled an undefined border region, smuggling was virtually a way of life for many in the Fundy area. Moreover, the practice of evading or circumventing both British and American Customs duties had been honed to a fine art during the period of on-again off-again embargoes and trade restrictions leading up to the War of 1812.

The shifting state of Maritime-American relations throughout the period of undeclared war in 1812 simply encouraged Fundy merchants and their American neighbours to develop even more ingenious ways of expanding their illicit trading relationships. For example, with so many privateers around, it was relatively easy for a New Brunswick ship loaded with British goods to sail out of Saint John or St. Andrews and by prearranged signal, be "captured" by an American privateer and carried into a nearby port as prize. When the goods were sold, the sender and the captor would split the profits and arrange to do it again. In July 1812, instructions for just such a false capture were found aboard the Boston privateer *Friendship*, seized by HMS *Indian* in the Bay of Fundy. The schooner was ordered to proceed to Saint John where "Mr. A" would make arrangements in a "most secret manner" for a New Brunswick vessel to be seized. Then, while keeping an eye out for both British and American vessels of war, the privateer was to set up a capture by firing two or three volleys "in a sham way." There was even a sketch of a triangular pennant in blue with a white X that the vessel was supposed to fly so that the "prize" would recognize her.

Without doubt, contraband American goods stealthily entered the province the same way. Although no letter of marque has been found for her, it is possible that the 39-ton schooner *Buckskin* might have been one of these dubious privateers. One of the numerous commerce raid-

"Signal for Collusive Capture," white on blue, found aboard the American privateer *Friendship*. (NAC RG 8, vol 122: "The *Friendship*")

ers launched out of Salem, Massachusetts, *Buckskin*'s first cruise lasted only a month before she and her prize were taken by Royal Navy vessels just off Halifax. Captured prior to Britain's declaration of war, she was condemned to the Crown rather than to her captors. Later, she was sold to St. Andrews interests and fitted out as a privateer with three guns and a crew of thirty. In June 1813, *Buckskin* is reported to have come under heavy fire from American militia forces on Fox Island while trying to retake several prizes. In one of the few references to loss of life aboard privateers, her captain and several others were said to have been killed and an officer wounded. After that she disappears from the record.

Because of the need for secrecy, there are no records concerning how many merchants on both sides of the border participated in false captures of each other's goods. One historian suggests that most privateer captures of American vessels in the Bay of Fundy and Passamaquoddy were probably pre-arranged shipments to merchants in Saint John and St. Andrews. Another historian estimates that up to a hundred merchants from New York and elsewhere participated in smuggling in Passamaquoddy Bay during Jefferson's earlier embargo against trade with the British. Like privateering, smuggling was a temporary activity that appealed to young, single men, who, in the case of American smugglers, had little to fear from the law. One of the main differences between the British and American prize rules was that Americans accused of Customs offenses were entitled to a jury trial. The remote likelihood that anyone in the District of Maine would be found guilty by his neighbours for evading Customs duties meant that few American smugglers ever went to trial.

In fact, under American law, evading Customs duties was illegal but the act of smuggling was not. On Moose Island, Maine, the American-owned warehouses in Eastport were not only larger than any in Saint John, but it was said that more business was conducted off the island in one day than went through Saint John in two months. And Moose Island was within a gunshot of the British-owned Campobello, Deer, Marvel and Indian Islands. With so many bays and inlets dotting the Bay of Fundy and the coast of Maine, it was virtually impossible for naval or Customs vessels from either side to keep track of the goods moving in and out in daylight let alone under cover of darkness.

One of the favourite tricks used by local smugglers was to find a secluded anchorage where they would transfer goods from British to American ships and vice versa. British manufactured goods were smuggled into the United States via Saint John and St. Andrews on a regular basis, thanks largely to corrupt or incompetent Customs officials. For example, it was William Wanton, New Brunswick's first Customs Collector, who decreed that the waters between Campobello Island and Moose Island should be declared neutral to facilitate trade. When he died in office in 1816 at age 82, Wanton's annual salary, including fees for every service connected with shipping, was £2900 — some £900 more per year than the Lieutenant-Governor earned. With Customs men unwilling or unable to stop the illegal trade, things became so bad in Saint John that in July 1814 the *New Brunswick Courier* carried a notice offering a reward for information leading to the arrest of whoever had stolen the royal coat of arms from over the Custom House door.

Such independence of action was not, of course, limited to government officials. Recovering from his unfortunate experience at the hands of Americans early in the war, David Owen arbitrarily declared his island, Campobello, exempt from New Brunswick law. It immediately became a thriving smuggling port where local vessels landed British goods so that they could be picked up by passing American "fishermen." A slightly more sophisticated technique involved obtaining papers from the local Swedish consul or a representative of another neutral country and changing the ship's registry. Under international law, making the ship neutral made the cargo neutral, allowing both to legally enter American ports. To facilitate this "neutral trade," Eastport lawyer Jonathan D. Weston became a Swedish vice-consul. Not everyone approved of the situation. Edward Winslow, one of the early Loyalist settlers in Saint John, was disgusted by the situation in Campobello and Moose Island, claiming "These islands are the asylum of deserters from the British navy and Army, criminals and absconding debtors from New Brunswick and Nova Scotia."

On the American side, where the revenue officers tended to be less corrupt, defrauding Customs took on a whole new dimension. A system of paying for information leading to ship seizures actually encouraged smugglers to anonymously inform against themselves, thereby getting Customs officers to bring their cargos safely into port for them. Once the cargo was in custody, "trustworthy" merchants or masters could post bond for a vessel to enable the smugglers to continue to trade while waiting for the case to go to court. Although the court appointed evaluators to estimate the value of the captured goods, many were friends of the merchants and appraised the goods well below market value. Thus a claimant not only paid a lower bond but he could buy back his own goods at auction for a fraction of their real value. If Customs made an arrest, the informant could apply to the courts for his twenty five per cent share from the sale of the seized goods, obtain a Customs certificate indicating that the goods had legally entered the United States, sell them openly and still make a profit. One of the most enthusiastic participants in this double game was Jabez Mowry of Eastport, who owned warehouses on both sides of the border. In the early years of the war, he is said to have smuggled $50,000 worth of beef and pork into Nova Scotia for the British troops in Halifax. He also supplied provisions for the American garrison on Moose Island and then reported on American troop strength to

the British commander at St. Andrews. Smuggling in the Bay of Fundy border region only ended when the British occupied northern Maine in the summer of 1814. When that happened many local Americans simply switched allegiances and carried on as loyal British subjects, while the smuggling problem just moved south to the Penobscot Bay area, where M'Waters and the sloop *Mary* got into trouble.

By hook and by crook, New Brunswickers turned the first six months following the American declaration of war to their advantage. Licences, letters of marque and illicit trade helped keep the provincial economy rolling through the undeclared war of June to October 1812. But by the time privateering was officially sanctioned, New Brunswick's reputation for bending the law was so bad that would-be privateers had to obtain their commissions from Nova Scotia.

*Opposite: Saint John from the Signal, 1841*, by Charles Cousen. Saint John was the home of most of New Brunswick's privateers and privateer owners during the War of 1812. (NBM)

## Chapter Two

# At War at Last: 1813-1814

When all efforts to restore peace by diplomatic means proved useless and with American armies attacking Upper and Lower Canada, the British government was finally forced to declare war. On October 13, 1812, about the time General Sir Isaac Brock earned fame for his defence of Queenston Heights along the Niagara frontier, the Prince Regent formally authorized letters of marque against the United States. British subjects along the eastern seaboard of North America could now officially engage in warfare.

As the war progressed and attacks by American privateers and the small but surprisingly feisty US Navy started to interfere with British shipping, the Royal Navy began to apply a tourniquet to American trade by blockading the main ports along the eastern seaboard. Beginning with Chesapeake Bay in December 1812, Admiral Warren, who had replaced Sawyer a few months earlier, gradually sealed off shipping southward from Rhode Island, closing the Potomac, James, York and Rapahannock Rivers. By March 1813, his ships had pushed to the Mississippi River. Although he put off securing New England ports until the last, by November 1813, Warren had succeeded in blockading some two thousand miles of coastline. This strategy struck at the heart of the American economy and went a long way toward turning American thoughts to peace.

But British naval actions in late 1812 had little impact on the Bay of Fundy, not least because war was not officially proclaimed in the colonies for several more months. As a result, at least two more New Brunswick vessels obtained letters of marque in what turned out to be a rather prolonged apprehended war. The first was the *Union*, a small vessel of one gun owned by George Younghusband, Samuel Miles, William R. Boyd and John Atkinson of Saint John. On November 20, 1812, Atkinson and William Ward, both merchants from Saint John, posted a £1500 bond for the vessel's good behaviour. Given its diminutive size and armament, *Union* was clearly meant to be an armed trader — a vessel concentrating on normal commerce but eligible to capture prizes of opportunity — rather than a privateer and does not appear to have captured any ships.

The other New Brunswick privateer from this period was the *Sir John Sherbrooke*, formerly the 187-ton American brigantine *Vernon*. She was purchased by brothers Robert and William Pagan and William Ritchie of Saint John, and outfitted as an armed trader with twelve guns and thirty men. Although the *Sir John Sherbrooke* was registered in New Brunswick, her bond was put up by Halifax merchants William Lawson, Enos Collins and Joseph Allison, who had interests in a number of Nova Scotia privateers. Commissioned the end of November 1812, under master Thomas Robson of Saint John, this first *Sir John Sherbrooke* seems to have made one trip to Jamaica via Bermuda and returned home in March 1813 without any prizes. In February 1813, the same Collins and Allison posted the bond for a second much more successful privateer named *Sir John Sherbrooke,* this one a 273-ton brigantine that had been the American privateer *Thorn* from Marblehead, Massachusetts. After March 1813, it was the Nova Scotian privateer, *Sir John Sherbrooke,* that brought in the prizes.

The first — and unsuccessful — privateer named *Sir John Sherbrooke* proved to be the last to receive a letter of marque from New Brunswick. By the middle of 1813, the Court of Vice-Admiralty had seen enough dubious captures and questionable privateering practices and received enough letters of complaint from aggrieved merchants to suggest that New Brunswick was either furnishing letters of a marque to phony privateers or her enthusiastic privateers were spoiling the traffic in smuggled goods. Whatever the reason, Lieutenant-Governor Smyth was forbidden to issue any more letters of marque.

Lieutenant-Governor John Coape Sherbrooke of Nova Scotia. Sherbrooke issued all letters of marque to New Brunswick-owned privateers after the power to do so was stripped from Lieutenant-Governor George S. Smyth of New Brunswick in early 1813. (NGC)

Undaunted, New Brunswickers simply obtained their letters of marque from Nova Scotia for the balance of the war. The original *Sir John Sherbrooke*, for example, under Captain Thomas Robson, continued in the lucrative West Indies trade as an armed trader under a letter of marque issued by Sir John Sherbrooke himself. There is no evidence that she captured any prizes, in fact she was eventually captured by American privateers. After departing Richibucto, New Brunswick, in October 1813, Robson vanished for several months until a letter from Kingston, Jamaica, dated December 12, 1813, reached the ship's owners. It is a matter-of-fact account of being attacked by an American brig-of-war, a packet and the Baltimore privateer, *Saucy Jack*. Robson and his tiny vessel held them off "at close action for one hour and thirty minutes," setting one vessel on fire twice while beating off three attempts to board him. *Sir John Sherbrooke* was on the point of escaping when Robson was shot in the head. He explained that his men had to give up the ship because the mate had already been wounded and "The nature of my wound was such as to prevent any service from me. The ball entering the mouth, passing out behind the left ear, which nearly caused my death." While three of his men were killed and four others wounded, the *Saucy Jack* had at least fifteen wounded and the American schooner was a complete wreck. Despite being outnumbered roughly five to one and nearly killed, Robson's one regret was being unable to save his ship.

## *Dart — The Pick of the Privateers*

New Brunswick's best known privateer, *Dart*, was also commissioned in Nova Scotia in early 1813. Duly famous for her impressive total of eleven prizes carried into port, *Dart* is also better known than her fellow privateers thanks to the survival of a set of Articles of Agreement signed by her crew and the log detailing her two cruises under Captain John Harris of Annapolis, Nova Scotia. Each privateer was obliged to keep a daily log or journal in which were recorded winds, weather, encounters with other ships and reports of any enemy activities. These logs could be reviewed

*The Action between His Majesty's Ship Shannon and the United States Frigate Chesapeake, off Boston Light House on the 1st of June 1813*, by John T. Lee, engraved by Joseph Jeakes. The capture of *Chesapeake*, on the left, cleared the way for two of *Dart*'s most successful cruises. (NAC C-007470)

by any Royal Navy vessels requesting it for intelligence or used in court cases arising from captures at sea. Unfortunately, few logs still survive, and that of the *Dart* is quite unique.

A 47-ton sloop, *Dart* was small for a privateer, but her four carronades — lightweight guns of large calibre, easily handled by a small crew and devastating at short range against wooden ships — two swivel guns and forty-five man crew made up for her lack of size. Originally the American privateer *Actress* from New Haven, Connecticut, she was captured by HMS *Spartan* on July 18, 1812. Once condemned, she sat in Saint John harbour until April 22, 1813, when she was auctioned off to her new owners, Robert Shives, John Hay Sr. and James Thorpe Hanford

Most small privateers carried cannons — long guns of considerable range but firing a fairly light ball — and lots of men. *Dart* and several others were equipped primarily with carronades like this 12-pounder mounted in the reconstructed blockhouse at Edmundston, New Brunswick. (NBMHP)

of Saint John. Intending to fit her out as a privateer, they first petitioned Lieutenant-Governor Sherbrooke of Halifax for permission to purchase guns and ammunition for the *Dart* from the provincial ordnance stores. Two weeks later they requested a letter of marque, and on May 4, 1813, *Dart* received her first commission.

After several weeks of rounding up provisions, equipment and a crew for his first cruise, Captain Harris was ready to make history. Before sailing, the men signed *Dart*'s ten Articles of Agreement accepting their conditions of work. Consisting of both landsmen and seamen according to the regulations for privateers, nearly half the crew had to make their marks because they could not write their names. Under Article 1, the owners' retained a claim on up to half of any prize money *Dart* earned in order to recoup their investment for arming and provisioning the privateer, after which they would share the remaining half with the ship's company. *Dart*'s 45-man crew agreed to share in any prizes as follows: the Commander received eight shares; the two First Lieutenants, five each; each of four prize masters (men qualified to take command of captured ships and bring them into port) received four shares; the boatswain or bosun, both gunners, the purser and the carpenter each got three shares with the bosun's and carpenter's mates receiving a lesser share; the sergeant of marines took two shares; the cook, steward and three able seamen got one and a half shares each; the seven landsmen got one share apiece and the five ship's boys each got three-quarters of a share. The remaining crew, ten seamen and three unidentified crew were presumably treated according to their rank.

The next few articles of *Dart*'s Agreement governed shipboard behaviour and included an agreement to serve for the full three months duration of the cruise, to obtain the commanding officer's permission to go ashore, to allow the captain to choose their cruising ground and to take stores for the ship out of their prizes without paying for them as long as the prize suffered no harm. Any man causing a disturbance on board, mutinying, behaving in a cowardly way or being drunk in action was promptly punished and forfeited his shares to the rest of the crew. Under Article 8, deserters forfeited their share of prize money, but instead of going to the crew, it went to the owners to pay for their replacements. To inspire the crew, the first man to spy the sail of an eventual prize was rewarded with one guinea (£1.1) while the first man to board a prize would receive £5 for bravery out of the gross sum of prize money. Another article provided for successive crew members to take over the ship in the event of the captain's death. The final article bound all the men, their heirs, executors and administrators in sum of £100 lawful money to abide by these articles.

*Dart*'s journal opens on Saturday, May 22, 1813 and records several days of gales and rain. With one eye on the weather and the other searching the horizon for sails, shipboard life for Captain Harris and his men seesawed between tedium and tension. On Friday, May 28, *Dart*'s boat chased the Eastport schooner *Sally* out of Little River only to discover that she was in ballast and had a licence. Disappointed and soon enveloped in "dark, thick weather," *Dart* fell in with a naval vessel, the 360-ton HMS *Rattler* escorting a prize back to Saint John. At two-thirty in the morning, thinking the American-built *Dart* was an enemy privateer, Captain Alexander Gordon, RN, fired two shots at her, hitting her below the waterline. Harris stopped immediately, and when Gordon realized his mistake, he sent over his ship's carpenter to help plug the hole.

For the next few days, often in "thick fogg," *Dart's* crew sailed slowly southward between the rocky islands along the coast of Maine, taking in water from the shot hole and looking for a safe place to fix the leak. By June 1, the weather had improved, and the leak was repaired in quiet waters northwest of Seal Rock, off Penobscot Bay. But in ten days of searching, all the privateer captured was a barrel of pork and some potatoes from a small chebaco (or jebacco) boat, the *Fair Play,* full of women passengers from Portsmouth, New Hampshire, to Eastport, and the little schooner *Joanna*. The schooner, under Captain Alex Newcombe of Martha's Vineyard, was apparently carrying a licensed cargo of fifteen hundred bushels of his own corn to Halifax. Mistaking *Dart* for the American privateer she had once been, Newcombe later claimed that he hid his British licence for fear he would be arrested for trading with the enemy. Once he was sure his captors were British, he tried to show them his licence. According to Newcombe's statement to the Vice-Admiralty Court, Harris not only refused to accept his licence, he claimed it was worth nothing and boasted that he would take all vessels worth sending in. When Newcombe objected and demanded to be taken to Saint John with his ship, Harris refused to give him passage and told him that "if he did not pull away from the Privateer he would sink the Boat in which he was." Meanwhile, Harris's log records that the master "made use of such threatening language that it was thought prudent to send him on shore." Regardless of who was telling the truth, the court awarded the prize to *Dart*.

That same day, further to the south, the British frigate HMS *Shannon* under Captain Phillip Broke, RN, lured the USS *Chesapeake* into

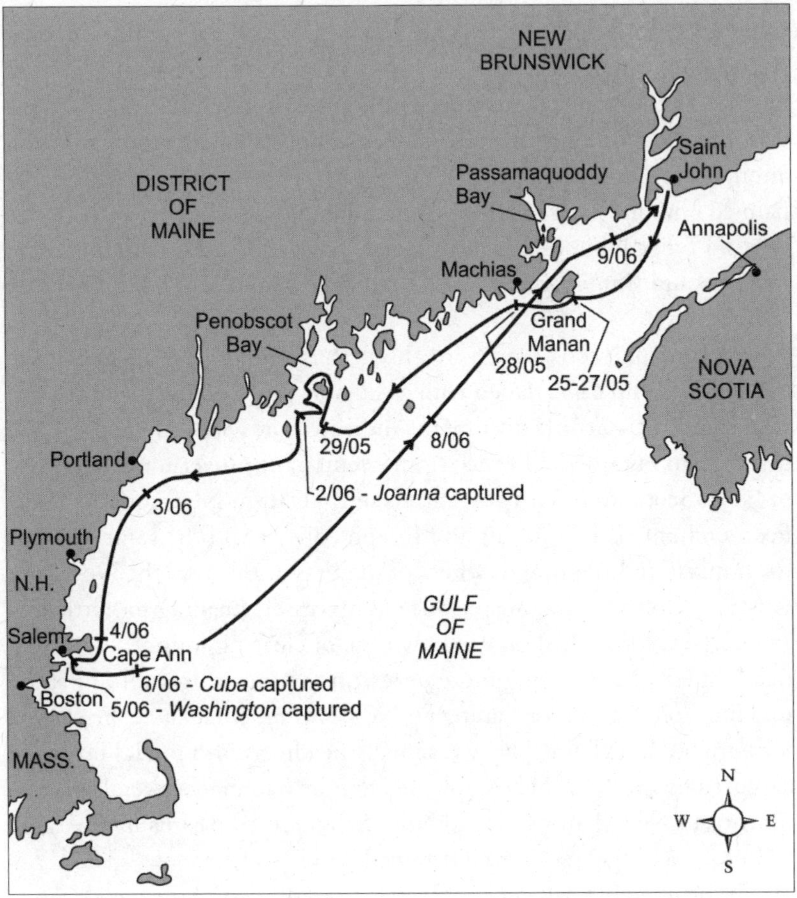


The cruise of the *Dart*, May 24 to June 10,1813, during which she brought home three prizes.

battle off Boston. Broke's frigate was the best gunnery ship in the Royal Navy, and after luring *Chesapeake* out for a duel, *Shannon* brought her opponent to a standstill with the first broadsided. The arrival of the two frigates in Halifax harbour was one of the most celebrated events of the war at sea against the Americans.

Harris learned of the capture of the *Chesapeake* off Cape Ann, Massachusetts, on June 4, and that cleared the waters off Boston for small privateers. On June 5, *Dart* seized her second prize off Salem: the schooner *Washington*, which Harris described as "a Beautiful Pilot Boat of 65 tons burthen entirely new pierced for Guns comfortably fitted, and I expect was intended for a privateer." She was stopped while in company with another Portland, Maine vessel, the *Superb*, a chebacco boat with a red-painted bow and a cargo of salt. After manning the schooner with a prize crew for Saint John, Harris put a female passenger along with the rest of *Joanna*'s and *Washington*'s crew aboard *Superb*, and sent her on her way to Baltimore.

On June 6, it took *Dart* a five-hour chase and two shots to capture the 176-ton ship *Cuba,* laden with a valuable cargo of flour, southeast of Cape Ann. Prize court documents indicate that David Bishop, *Cuba*'s owner, had obtained a licence from Lieutenant-Governor Sherbrooke of Nova Scotia to import 750 barrels of flour from New York for Halifax merchants Enos Collins and Joseph Allison and the same amount for himself and the other owners of the vessel. Because the New York Customs Collector was suspicious of any vessels heading to northeastern ports, Captain Bishop used the trick of clearing for one port while heading for another lying more or less in the same direction. First, he told the Collector he was sailing for New Haven. Once there, he cleared for Portland but claimed he was actually heading north to Halifax when captured by the *Dart.* He complained that he had made several successful trips to New Brunswick and Nova Scotia in the past using the same technique and had never been detained.

Unfortunately for Bishop, affidavits from the rest of the crew contradicted his statement. One witness, Henry Gibbs, swore that the *Cuba* was steering directly and steadily for Portland. Helmsman John Joe, "a subject of the King of Spain," admitted he was steering the vessel at the time but "does not know where the said ship was when taken." Seaman Anthony Carbell fully expected to land in Portland the next morning, while *Cuba*'s cook, Charles Dyer, had no idea where they were heading. Although Neapolitan seaman Nicholas Bart thought they were heading to Portland, he wasn't really sure because he didn't understand navigation and had just been "taken out of Gaol in New Haven and came away

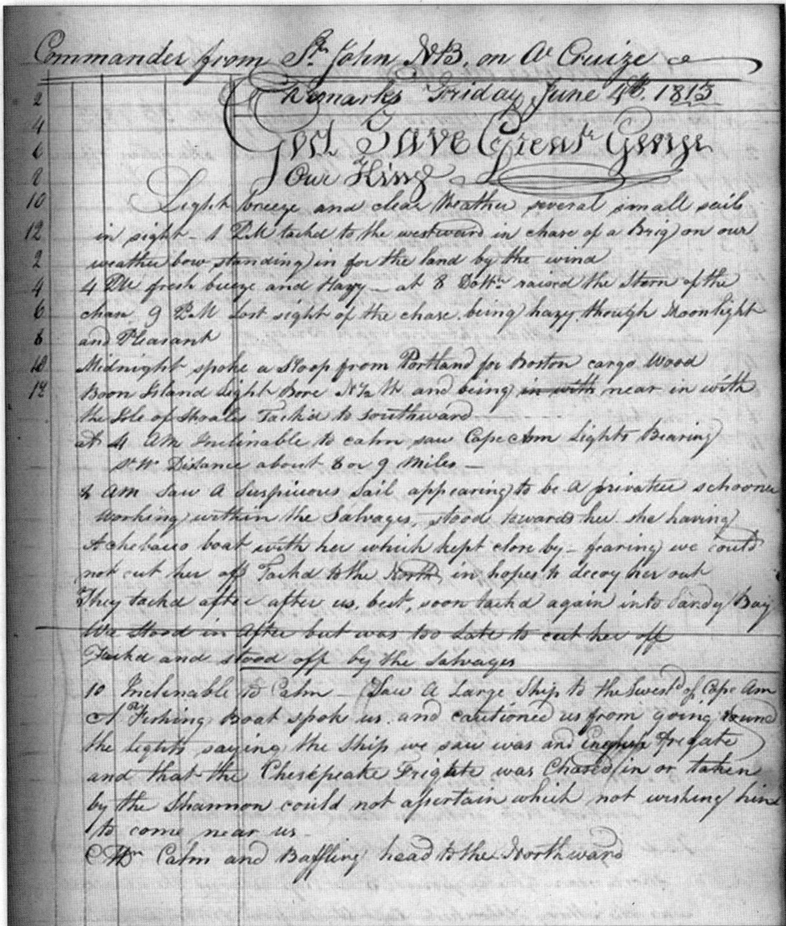

Commander from St. John N.B. on a Cruize

Remarks Friday June 4th 1813

God Save Great George Our King

Light breeze and clear weather several small sails in sight - 1 P.M. tacked to the westward in chase of a Brig on our weather bow standing in for the land by the wind
4 P.M. fresh breeze and Hazy - at 8 Do. raised the Stern of the chase 9 P.M. Lost sight of the chase being hazy through Moonlight and Pleasant
Midnight spoke a Sloop from Portland for Boston cargo Wood Boon Island Light Bore N½W and being ~~in with~~ near in with the Isle of Shoals Tacked to southward
At 4 AM Inclinable to calm saw Cape Ann Lights Bearing SW Distance about 8 or 9 Miles -
8 AM saw a Suspicious Sail appearing to be a privateer schooner working within the Salvages, stood towards her she having A chebacco boat with her which kept close by - fearing we could not cut her off Tacked to the North in hopes to decoy her out They tacked afte after us, but, soon tacked again into Sandy Bay
~~We stood in after but was too late to cut her off~~
Tacked and stood off by the Salvages
10 Inclinable to Calm - Saw a Large Ship to the Swest of Cape Ann A Fishing Boat spoke us and cautioned us from going round the lights saying the Ship we saw was an English Frigate and that the Chesapeake Frigate was Chased in or taken by the Shannon could not ascertain which not wishing him to come near us
Mdn Calm and Baffling head to the Northward

Log of the *Dart* for June 4, 1813, the day Captain Harris learned of the capture of the USS *Chesapeake*. (DUA)

the same day." Confused by so many different versions of their supposed destination from the captured crew, the judge finally awarded the prize to *Dart*.

Harris and the *Dart* returned to Saint John on June 9, with *Washington* in company and having joined *Cuba* at the landfall of Musquash Head: and so *Dart* entered harbour with two of her three prizes. The

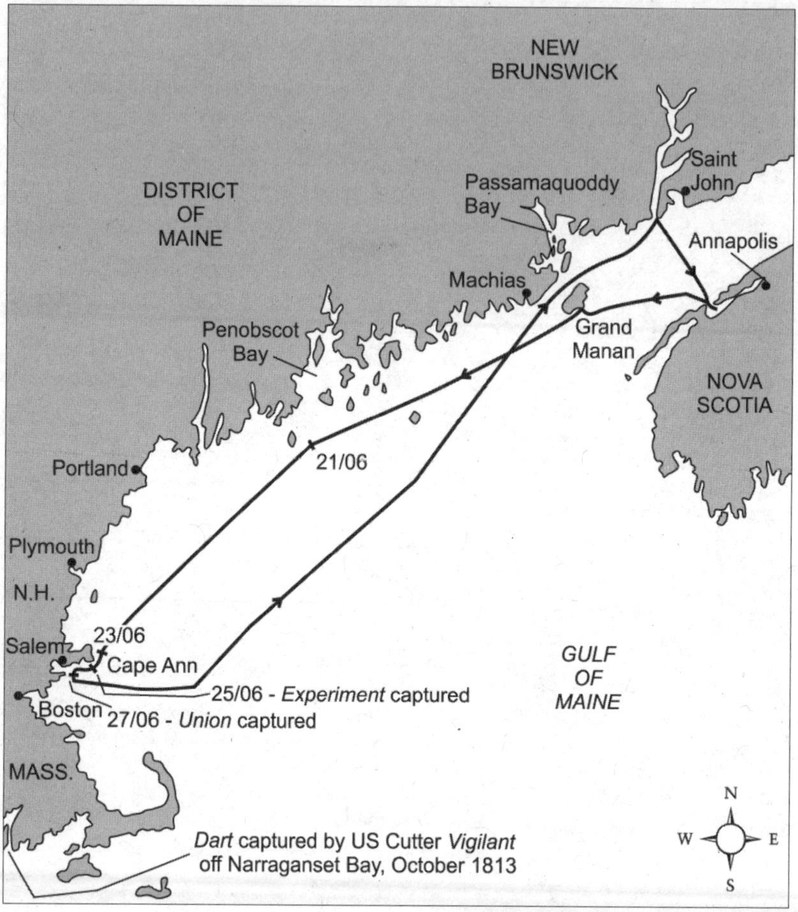


The cruise of the *Dart*, June 16-30, 1813. Her previous success off Cape Ann prompted a direct return to that area, with nearly as much luck.

next eight days were spent working on the ship and trying to keep his crew sober and obedient. Finally, on June 17, Harris sailed for his own home port of Annapolis, Nova Scotia, to get his ship in order, "the Crew Sober and some more Officers." A few days later, back at sea after a brief stop at Grand Manan, the *Dart* made straight for Cape Ann again. Harris reported keeping all hands busy, and presumably sober, "making Baggs for Grape Shot, swivel shot, Pouches for Cartridges &c Carpenter fitting pumps - Boatswain and Crew at the rigging."

On Friday, June 25, after rejecting a couple of merchantmen out of Boston, Harris' men captured a small coasting sloop, *Experiment*, whose cargo of rum, ginger, sugar, tobacco and coffee was worth sending in. The next few days Harris boarded and released half a dozen vessels without making a prize. Finally, while still cruising off Cape Ann about sunset on Sunday, June 26, he spied a fast-sailing ship with eight guns per side. Suspecting her to be a captured English vessel with a small prize crew aboard, he prepared his ship for action. Luckily, it only required one shot from the *Dart's* bow gun to bring her to. Nearly four times *Dart's* size, the 230-ton *Union* was carrying a cargo of salt, fruit and block tin from Cadiz, Spain, to Boston. The captain readily produced a licence signed by General Wellesley (later the Duke of Wellington) in charge of the British forces in Spain, but Harris thought the tin might be considered an article of war, making it subject to seizure in spite of the licence. Although Harris lost the gamble and the *Union* was eventually restored to its owners, he felt justified in escorting it into Saint John and letting the Vice-Admiralty Court decide. Having won more than he lost, on Wednesday, June 30, Harris moored the *Dart* in Saint John harbour and wrote: "Thus ends the Cruize with the *Dart*."

Under international law, a letter of marque applied only for the duration of the licensed cruise or until the master, owners, armament or other key aspect of the commission changed. A new letter of marque dated July 14, 1813, indicates that James Ross, Harris's second in command on the *Dart's* first cruise, had taken over as captain of the privateer. The third and final cruise of the *Dart* began with mixed success and ended in a bloody skirmish with a US revenue cutter. *Dart's* first two prizes were Maine coastal vessels, the ship *Mequait* out of Bath laden with corn, rye and fish, and the schooner *Dolphin*, heading from Portland to Boston with a load of cordwood. A third prize, the Cape Ann coasting schooner *Three Brothers,* was taken a week later.

At the end of August, Ross seized the Boston schooners *Hero* and *Camden*, but since both were in ballast, neither earned the *Dart's* crew much in the way of prize money. By law, privateers were required to bring back a member of the captured crew to answer questions concerning the capture, but *Camden*'s master begged Ross to land them nearby because both he and the mate were sick and he didn't want to abandon his young nephew who was with them. Although Ross claimed that he had landed the crew on Wood Island in response to their pleas, he probably did not have enough men left to make up a prize crew anyway. Lack of crew may have contributed to the loss of another prize. As reported in Saint John's *Royal Gazette*, *Dart* had captured a schooner off Mount Desert, Maine, put on a two-man prize crew and left an eighteen-year-old from the original crew aboard to act as pilot. While sailing north in thick fog, the pilot deliberately headed the vessel into Machias harbour where it was recaptured by the local revenue cutter. Another story in the *Boston Gazette* reported that the *Dart* had been sighted off Wood Island for several days but had finally headed home because she had manned out so many prizes there were only seven or eight men left on board. Ross' last prize to make it to court was the 49-ton schooner *Deborah*, seized on September 1 while carrying corn, apples and salt to Saco, Maine. After court costs and expenses were paid, the net sales of the vessel and cargo amounted to just over £150, hardly a rich prize when split between the owners and forty-five men.

*Dart*'s career as a privateer finally ended in early October 1813. According to an article in the *Essex Register* of Salem, Massachusetts, the behaviour of Captain Ross and his crew seems to have taken a piratical turn. Falling in with the merchant vessel *Governor Strong,* off Point Judith, at the entrance to Narragansett Bay, Rhode Island, Captain Ross not only detained her for seven hours, but treated the captain and passengers "in a most rascally manner." Ross was accused of threatening to put them in irons and sending the ship to Halifax, even though he admitted that the capture probably wouldn't stand up in court. Finally, after pointing a loaded pistol at Captain Smith and offering to shoot him and the rest of the passengers, Captain Ross stole five hundred dollars in cash and let *Governor Strong* go on its way. The Americans soon sounded the alarm, and the Revenue Cutter *Vigilant* lying nearby set off to capture the privateer. Armed with four 12-pound guns, two long guns firing 6-pound shot and six swivel guns with 2-pound shot, *Vigilant* was more than a match for *Dart* — especially at long range, beyond the reach of *Dart*'s carronades. Both ships exchanged fire as the cutter approached. While the *Vigilant* was undamaged, the unfortunate first Lieutenant of the privateer was cut in half by a 6-pound cannonball (roughly the size of a baseball) while at the helm. The only other casualty was a boy from the *Vigilant* who was thought to have fallen between the vessels during the boarding and drowned.

Drawing alongside, the cutter's men prepared to board the *Dart* whereupon the remaining twenty-two privateers and their officers are said to have begged for quarter, deserted their posts and fled below decks without further resistance. No sooner had the Americans taken possession of the vessel than Captain Ross emerged from the cabin, seized a musket and shot the sentry posted over the main hatch through the right arm. After this cowardly and dishonourable act against the men to whom his ship had surrendered, Ross blatantly denied having stolen any money from the *Governor Strong*. Unconvinced, *Vigilant*'s captain made Ross open his trunk where he found the five hundred dollars, which the grateful owners shared among the cutter's crew. The final insult, according to the Salem newspaper was that the terrible commander of the *Dart* was said to have been born in the United States. In a much less libelous tone, the Saint John *Royal Gazette* of October 19 merely reported the capture of the privateer *Dart* by an unnamed revenue cutter who carried her into Portland. The career of New Brunswick's most successful privateer was over.

## *Star, Hare, Herald and Snapdragon*

Following in the *Dart*'s wake in August 1813, Nehemiah Merritt and others from Saint John petitioned Lieutenant-Governor Sherbrooke for a letter of marque for the schooner *Star*. Her captain was twenty-six-year-old Caleb Seeley of Saint John, a tall, handsome sailor who went on to become one of the most successful privateer captains in Canadian history when he later commanded the Nova Scotia ship the *Liverpool Packet*. During his twenty-two day cruise in *Star* in the late summer of 1813, Seeley took at least three prizes, although none earned his owners enough to persuade them to continue investing. The first prize was the sloop *Elizabeth* taken at anchor and in ballast on August 25 near Moose Island. A week later, *Star* took the 58-ton sloop *Resolution* laden with iron ore ballast worth less than £400. The last prize was the fishing schooner *Flower* which was bought in December by *Star*'s owner and later sold for £175.

Following his success in the *Star*, Caleb Seeley invested some of his prize money as part owner and master of the *Liverpool Packet*. By the time Seeley took command of the famous privateer, she had already earned a reputation for success. She had been captured by the Royal Navy before the war for slave trading and was lying in Halifax when a group of locals bought her and outfitted the sleek, fast ship for privateering. Under Captain John Barss, the *Liverpool Packet* became the scourge of the New England coast by early 1813, and her capture in June by the American privateer *Thomas* of Portsmouth, New Hampshire, was a much celebrated event. In fact, the Americans turned her around, dubbed her the *Portsmouth Packet* and sent the schooner back into the Bay of Fundy to prey on British shipping. It was there that she was recaptured by HMS *Fantome* in October 1813, then repurchased by her original owner's Enos Collins of Halifax and Benjamin Knaut and James and John Barss of Liverpool, and recommissioned as a privateer under her old name.

Seeley took command of the *Liverpool Packet* in December 1813 and spent that month cruising solo off Cape Cod. In January 1814, he returned to the entrance to Long Island Sound in company with another Nova Scotia privateer, the *Retaliation*. By the time he was finished, Seeley sent in at least fourteen prizes in eleven months earning the respect of both his fellow privateers and his foes. He was particularly noted for his courage, fairness in the treatment of prisoners and being a gentleman. Under his command, the *Liverpool Packet* once again became the subject

New Brunswick's most famous privateer, Caleb Seeley. Born in Saint John in 1787 to Loyalist parents, Seeley used his profits from the *Star* to invest in the *Liverpool Packet* of Nova Scotia, British North America's most successful privateer. He then commanded her in 1813-1814, capturing fourteen more prizes. After the war Seeley settled in Liverpool, Nova Scotia, becoming a distinguished citizen and dying at the age of eighty-two in 1869. (QCM)

of legends and the scourge of the New England coast. Caleb Seeley was also the most successful privateer in New Brunswick history.

Others were either not as skilled, nor as lucky. As the owners of the New Brunswick privateers *Herald, Hare* and *Snapdragon* discovered, carrying letters of marque from Nova Scotia did not improve their success in 1813. The 300-ton *Herald* was originally the large American privateer *York Town* of New York, carrying eighteen guns and 160 men. She was captured by the Royal Navy in July 1813 and purchased by merchants Hugh Johnson and Son and Thomas Milledge of Saint John. Michael Tobin of Halifax and William McDonald of Saint John put up her bond. The largest of New Brunswick's privateers, she was outfitted as a letter of marque trader in early September 1813, with only ten guns and twenty-five crew under Charles Simmonds. She does not appear to have sent in any prizes before her career was cut short by a late November gale. While en route to Jamaica, *Herald* was cast away and lost on Eastern Wolfe Island, New Brunswick, less than ten miles from St. Andrews. The November 30 edition of the Saint John *Royal Gazette* reported her loss but was able to reassure readers that all the crew, except Jeremiah Prescott, were saved. Her owners survived the loss as well. Thomas Milledge later moved to Nova Scotia, represented Digby in the Nova Scotia House of Assembly and served as a judge in the provincial Inferior Court of Common Pleas. Captain Simmonds not only survived the war but went on to become the Speaker of the New Brunswick House of Assembly.

*Hare* was also an ex-American privateer, the *Wasp* of Salem. She was much smaller and only marginally more successful than *Herald*. Her owners, Noah Disbrow, John Clark and Hugh Doyle, all from Saint John, obtained a letter of marque for the 38-ton sloop from Lieutenant-Governor Sherbrooke on November 29, 1813. *Hare*'s first cruise under Captain James Reid produced no prizes. With Captain Samuel Godsoe in command in January 1814, she took two prizes, the sloop *Hero* laden with cordwood and the brig *Recovery*. Returning to Castine, Maine, after a six-month trading voyage in the Caribbean, the master of the brig only discovered that the port was embargoed when *Hare* attempted to board her. Although *Recovery* had been carrying some cash on board, before the privateer could take possession of her, the mate grabbed the money, hoisted it into the longboat and escaped to shore.

*Hare*'s last cruise, as noted in the *Boston Patriot* of March 9, 1814, ended dramatically and badly. The story comes from a journal kept by the captain of the US Revenue Cutter *Income* stationed at Machias, Maine. Captain Daniel Elliot (formerly captain of the *Commodore Barry,* which became the *Brunswicker*) was lying at Moosepecky Head harbour on February 22 when he observed a sail that turned out to be the *Hare*. Using his boat as a decoy, Elliott sent most of his ten man crew on shore to attack the *Hare*'s men when they rowed over to seize what Captain Godsoe thought was an American privateer run ashore. Although they managed to get the prize off the shore, *Hare*'s crew struck a ledge and were unable to get free before they were ambushed by Elliot's men and some local inhabitants of Sawyer's Cove. Two of *Hare*'s men were wounded and eventually captured. For a couple of hours Godsoe tacked back and forth, firing his two guns and trying to make a capture, but he finally had to sail away empty-handed. *Hare* never sailed as a privateer again.

New Brunswick's last privateer, the 160-ton Baltimore clipper *Snapdragon,* was a famous privateer in her own right. Operating from New Bern, North Carolina, the *Snap-Dragon* sent in prizes worth somewhere between $250,000 and two million dollars — accounts vary widely. Her enterprising commander, Captain Otway Burns, was reckoned to be one of the state's naval heroes and lies buried in a stone crypt with one of *Snap-Dragon*'s guns mounted on top. Her career as an American privateer ended in June 1814, when she was captured by the sloop HMS *Martin*. The firm of Curry and Hanford of Saint John purchased her shortly afterwards, rechristened her *Snapdragon* and sent her off to hunt the dwindling American merchant fleet.

There are two letters of marque recorded for the *Snapdragon* in 1814, one for August 9 and one for November 11. Bail for her last cruise was posted by merchants John Roy and Samuel Cunard of Halifax who had

*Capture of Snap Dragon*, by Irwin John Bevan, June 30, 1814. Rechristened *Snapdragon*, the ship became New Brunswick's last privateer. (MM)

done the same for the *Dart*. Following a first cruise without a prize, Captain James Reid, Godsoe's predecessor on the *Hare*, took her out a second time but could not change her luck before the war ended in December 1814.

## *Alternatives to Privateering*

As trade dried up along the American coast, it brought with it rising prices for scarce commodities, food shortages, unemployment and serious hardship for many. Since there are no prizes on record for New Brunswick-owned vessels during 1814, it would appear that the British blockade and an increased naval presence in the Bay of Fundy effectively put an end to New Brunswick's privateering activity, both real and arranged. Smuggling and illegal trade still persisted in and around the coast of Maine until British naval forces captured Eastport without a shot in July 1814. Interestingly, all the town's inhabitants took an oath of allegiance to the King, including the deacon of the church, "a smooth-tongued man accounted one of the sleekest smugglers." A month later, the nearby port of Castine fell, putting the territory from the Penobscot

River to the Canadian border under British control and eliminating the need to smuggle.

Over the years, enterprising merchants on both sides of the border had managed to move goods over land and sea in spite of whatever restrictions were being enforced at the time. By the summer of 1814, with the entire coast of America under blockade, virtually the entire overseas trade of the United States was conducted with British licences through British ports, using British middlemen and lining the pockets of the British crown. The integration of American trade into the British system prompted Sir George Prevost, Governor-General of Canada, to complain that two-thirds of the British army in Canada were eating American beef. The fact that the British army and navy paid for their supplies with scarce cash ensured that such cross-border cooperation would continue — and that the United States fought the war with British gold.

Throughout the War of 1812, privateering, smuggling and counterfeit captures offered short-term solutions to the larger problem of restricted wartime trade while generating significant commercial activity. But capturing enemy vessels involved so many hazards with such an unreliable return on investment that the majority of New Brunswick's maritime community preferred to make their living by ordinary means, if at all possible. While it may not have played a major role in the outcome of the war, privateering did provide an economic outlet for those sailors, ship owners and merchants who chose to participate in it. The newspaper reports of captures and recaptures raised the morale of people who had to put up with wartime shortages and deal with the occasional loss of friends and loved ones to battles or storms at sea.

By the time representatives of Great Britain and the United States signed the Treaty of Ghent on Christmas Eve 1814, however, both sides were heartily sick of fighting. Nearly three years of unwanted war were followed by a peace where nobody won. "Free Trade and Sailors Rights" had ceased to be an issue before war was even declared. Whatever else people fought for, the treaty granted no new territory to either side and the British evacuation of northern Maine left the final decision regarding the Maine-New Brunswick border for another day. Unpopular and inconclusive, the War of 1812 nevertheless generated a certain amount of prosperity and self-confidence for New Brunswick and set the province up for the dramatic social, industrial and political changes of the mid-nineteenth century.

## Chapter Three

# The Chesapeake Affair, 1863-1864

New Brunswick prospered after 1815, thanks to the steady economic progress that had begun a decade or so earlier. Political struggles marked its development from military-based rule to an increasingly more responsible government. Maine attained statehood in 1820, and as their populations grew during the 1830s and forties, province and state jostled with each other for territory. The Webster-Ashburton Treaty of 1842 not only marked the first attempt to define the boundaries between the US and British territories, it also sought to suppress the African slave trade and deal with fugitives from justice, in certain cases. Enacted in Canada in 1843, it was partly successful in resolving the Maine-New Brunswick boundary dispute by confirming the St. John River as the natural east-west dividing line. However, since establishing the northern boundary necessitated ceding some Quebec property to Maine, this was not settled until the mid-1850s. By then, it seemed that the former conspirators-turned-competitors could finally return to being neighbours. New Brunswick's privateering experience was no longer needed when money could be made peacefully. Realizing that steam-powered national navies and ironclad hulls had made private armed vessels irrelevant, most European nations signed the 1856 Treaty of Paris, which effectively ended privateering.

Since the United States was one of the few countries that did not sign the Treaty of Paris, when the Civil War erupted in 1861 both the Union and Confederate governments were quick to issue letters of marque. For the Confederacy, privateering was really their only alternative, since virtually all of the US Navy remained in the hands of the North, and it was not long before the Union established a very effective strangle hold over Southern ports. It was privateers like the *Jefferson Davis* and sleek, high-speed blockade runners like the steam packet *Nashville (*later CSS *Rattlesnake)* that were able to evade the northern blockade. As the war progressed, many more of the larger privateers were taken over by the developing navy of the Confederate states and commissioned as proper warships, although that did not change their main objective of disrupting Northern commerce. In the meantime, in order to keep its economy afloat the South conducted a brisk traffic between ports in the Confederacy and the Caribbean and Europe. Cotton, especially, was shipped to British ports to supply the vast textile factories in the Midlands that now depended on the American resource. In return, high value cargoes — including weapons and munitions, diplomats and ready cash — flowed back. For many reasons, not least economic, much of British sentiment lay with the South. That support was inflamed early in the war when a US Navy patrol stopped the British steamer *Trent* on the high-seas in late 1861 and boldly removed two Confederate diplomats. For several months Great Britain and the US teetered on the brink of war, prompting the largest, and last, great movement of imperial troops through New Brunswick to help preserve the Canadas in the event of an American invasion. By spring 1862, the tensions had dissipated, but to many Northerners, Britain's pro-Southern tendencies remained suspect.

Whatever their political leaning, British merchants were quite happy to sell to both sides during the Civil War, although many of the most successful Confederate raiders and blockade runners were either built or purchased in Britain. The most famous of these was the 1016-ton steam-sail auxiliary schooner *Alabama,* which set off from Birkenhead in northwestern England in August 1862 on her sea trials and failed to return. She turned up several days later in the Azores, where she was armed with guns from Liverpool and put into commission in the Confederate Navy. Under the redoubtable Captain Raphael Semmes, *Alabama* preyed on Union shipping for nearly two years, destroying twenty-seven northern vessels in her first three months at sea. Her unique combination of both steam power and a full sailing rig enabled *Alabama* to reserve her precious coal supplies for battle while enjoying almost unlimited cruising under sail. By the time for she was cornered by the SS *Kearsarge* and sunk in battle off Cherbourg, France, in June 1864, this most successful Confederate raider had destroyed seventy-one Northern ships.

Like the rest of British North America, New Brunswickers watched anxiously as their neighbours to the south descended into a prolonged war of attrition. Even though it was illegal for a British subject to join the armed forces of another country, many young men and at least one woman, Sarah Emma Edmonds, who fought as a man, eagerly put on the blue Yankee uniform. Although most Maritimers seem to have joined the Union cause, they were probably motivated more by proximity than politics, combined with a desire for adventure or escape.

Neutral by law and inclination, New Brunswick would have had very little direct connection with the Civil War if it had not been for the *Chesapeake* affair of 1863: a bizarre "Confederate" plot that could have had serious repercussions for Britain and Canada. Although little more than a comic opera farce, the adventure generated electrifying headlines, set legal precedents and involved imprisonment, murder and piracy, narrow escapes and an international incident near Halifax. Given the earnest desire of both Great Britain and the United States to avoid anything that would inflame tensions and lead to war, the *Chesapeake* affair nonetheless ranks as one of the important — and virtually unknown — border incidents between British North America and the United States during the Civil War. A comparable incident in October 1865, the so-called St. Alban's raid, is enshrined in literature as the key manifestation of Confederate use of British soil to launch attacks on the Union from behind. In that instance, thirteen Confederate agents slipped across the border into Vermont and raided a bank before returning to Canada. Detained in Montreal and held for extradition, the men were released on a technicality. The decision angered American officials and is generally believed to have contributed to the climate of fear that helped propel Upper and Lower Canada into union with the Atlantic provinces a couple of years later.

But the St. Alban's raid was not the first such incident. The *Chesapeake* affair of 1863 set a precedent for agents acting from British soil against the

Union and then escaping justice under the British legal system. In fact, the incident was closely followed by the contemporary press, which published lurid details of the capture, the subsequent pursuit by the US Navy and the court cases. By the time it was over, the Confederacy had formally denied involvement with any of the conspirators let alone their dubious privateering commission. Even though the capture of the *Chesapeake* had absolutely no effect on the outcome of the Civil War, the legal and political turmoil it created infuriated the Northern states, upset the British Colonial and Foreign Offices, caused the Confederate government a certain amount of anxiety and heated up the telegraph lines between Washington and Halifax. Among the many legal issues it engendered was the first extradition case argued in New Brunswick under the Webster-Ashburton Treaty of 1842 that settled the New Brunswick-Maine boundary dispute. What was unique about the *Chesapeake* affair was that the gang of "Confederate" conspirators was composed almost entirely of New Brunswickers — and in the end, despite their hijacking of an American coastal steamer at sea in the name of the Confederacy, they all got off scot-free.

## *The Brain behind the Confederate Plotters*

The scheme to capture the *Chesapeake*, a New York-to-Portland steam-powered liner, for the Confederacy, rename her *Retribution* and sail her south to Wilmington, North Carolina, was hatched by a twenty-three-year-old illustrator aptly named John Clibbon Brain. It is significant to his story that his family emigrated from Britain and settled in Ohio in the 1850s. Whether Brain ever actually became a US citizen is unclear, but he was known to speak with an English accent when required and was later disowned by both North and South alike as a British subject. What is clear, however, is that Brain harboured Southern sympathies. By the time the Civil War broke out in 1861, he was a gunnery trainee in the Southern army. Disliking army life, he joined the Confederate Navy at Hampton Roads, Virginia, as an able seaman aboard the CSS *Jamestown*. According to letters he wrote to his British relatives, Brain witnessed the first famous battle between the ironclads *Monitor* and *Merrimac* in March

1862. More importantly, he also acquired a taste for steam propulsion and the desire to command his own vessel one day.

When the naval base and the *Merrimac* had to be abandoned to advancing Union forces, Brain was reluctant to return to artillery duty or the army. Instead, he volunteered to join the Confederate secret service, known as the Knights of the Golden Circle, and quickly rose to the rank of Lieutenant. Brain used his drawing skills to get a job preparing "Illustrated Railway Guides" as a cover for his work for the Confederacy. When captured and committed to a Massachusetts prison, he talked his way out by promising to leave the United States. Finding himself in Montreal without any money, Brain used his wartime experience and his wits. According to an article in the *Quebec Mercury*, Brain's next scheme involved posing as the representative of a Montreal publisher collecting subscriptions for a "Grand Trunk Railway Guide." During the summer of 1863, Brain collected enough money for the never-to-be-published guide from the merchants of Montreal and Quebec City that he could afford to continue his imposture in Liverpool and Manchester before his reputation finally caught up with him and he had to sail back to Virginia and the war.

By 1863, the Union Navy had Confederate shipping almost totally blockaded, and desperate schemes to break the blockade or disrupt the North's war at sea were not unusual. In June of that year, an enterprising Confederate naval officer named Lt. Charles W. Read slipped into the harbour in Portland, Maine, aboard the prize schooner *Archer*. He planned to capture the US Revenue Cutter *Caleb Cushing*, burn all ships in the harbour and get away before dawn. As it was, Read barely managed to get hold of the cutter and escape. Union forces in Portland responded quickly, and Read was only twenty miles out to sea when he was intercepted by two fast steamers — one of them being the New York-to-Portland liner *Chesapeake*, which was armed with two 6-pounder guns. Read fought until the *Caleb Cushing* ran out of ammunition, then set her afire, set a train to the powder magazine and ordered his men off. They were rescued by the other steamer, *Forest City,* as the cutter blew up.

Read's ill-fated capture of the *Caleb Cushing* in Portland in June 1863 may have been the inspiration for John C. Brain's next scheme. Although

Brain wanted to rejoin the navy, he knew his chances of gaining command of a Southern vessel were remote. Privateers and blockade runners were the only traffic in and out of southern ports so that seemed to be his best bet. But they were few in number and highly prized commands. In the meantime, Brain had reconnected with some of his earlier navy friends, among them former-Lieutenant Henry A. Parr, originally from Canada West, who became Brain's second in command. Parr's past was as shadowy as Brain's — he is described as either an "ex-doctor" or "an apothecary's unemployed apprentice."

Brain's plan was nothing if not daring. It involved seizing the same ship that had thwarted Read, the 460-ton liner *Chesapeake* in Northern-controlled waters right out from under the captain and crew, and then using a letter of marque from a defunct Lake Erie tugboat to turn the steamship into a commerce-raiding vessel under the Confederate flag. Whether condoned by his government or not, Brain's plan had a major legal flaw. A letter of marque granted to one ship could not legally be transferred to another, even if the new vessel changed names to match the commission.

The man with the letter of marque was Vernon Guyon Locke, a native of Shelburne, Nova Scotia, who had lived for 20 years in Fayetteville, North Carolina. Another shady character, Locke had purchased a derelict hull from the Southern navy, patched it up, converted it from steam to sail, renamed it the *Retribution* and obtained a privateering commission signed by Confederate Secretary of State, Judah Benjamin. For whatever reason, the commission was in the name of John Parker, apparently an alias of Locke's. When he eventually had to abandon the vessel in the Bahamas, Parker/Locke kept the letter of marque "just in case." Although it is not known what brought them together, by late Fall 1863, Locke, Brain and Parr had slipped through the Union lines and begun rounding up a crew.

New Brunswick was clearly the best place to stage such a scheme. The port of Saint John was — unlike Halifax — big, bustling and commercial: an easy place to secretly raise a crew and hatch their plans. In

Market Slip, Saint John, ca. 1865, a fruitful recruiting ground for the conspirators in the *Chesapeake* Affair. (NBM)

November 1863, the three men held a number of recruiting meetings in the back streets of Carleton, across the harbour from Saint John. Locals Charles Waiters, John Ring and James Trecarten, who attended meetings but did not join the crew, testified later that the plan was to go to New York and capture a vessel. Brain promised the men free passage to New York, the protection of a Confederate letter of marque, a share in all prizes from the Confederate government, arms to protect themselves (a pistol, ammunition and a set of irons to be picked up at a New York address) and a bonus of $500 if the steamer safely ran the blockade into Wilmington. Once theirs, *Chesapeake* would assume *Retribution*'s privateer identity and head south to prey on federal shipping.

According to later stories in the Saint John *Daily Evening Globe*, Locke stayed behind in New Brunswick while the crew of "ruffians, cowardly schemers" and "jailbirds" set off for New York. They included Brain, Parr as First Lieutenant, David Collins of Saint John as Second Lieutenant, George Robinson of St. Stephen as sailing master, and hands

Linus Seely (Carleton), James McKinley (Spruce Cove), George Wade (Loch Lambent), H.C. Brooks, Robert Clifford, brothers Gilbert and Robert Cox, two brothers called Moore and Isaac Treadwell from Saint John. In all, eleven of the so-called privateers were New Brunswickers. As they set sail from Saint John on December 2, their instructions were, "Use your own discretion as to the proper time and place of capture. Your actions toward crew and passengers will be strictly in accordance with the President's instructions."

## *The Chesapeake*

The *Chesapeake* was a propeller-driven steamship with one deck, three masts, a single funnel and a top speed of about eleven knots. In addition to ferrying passengers and freight between New York and Portland, she was also well known along the coast for her role in retaking the *Caleb Cushing*. Dismissed by the *Acadian Recorder* as a "miserable looking vessel." she had a rounded stern and carved head. She carried a coasting licence and a mixed cargo of flour, sugar, wine, leather and other goods consigned by merchants from Quebec, Nova Scotia and New Brunswick as well as New York. The value of the ship was estimated at $60,000 and the value of her cargo during that ill-fated voyage in early December 1863 ranged around $80,000. Her armament consisted of two 6-pounders, half a keg of powder and several revolvers but no cutlasses. She carried thirty tons of coal aboard, enough for the roughly thirty-six-hour trip to Portland. There were twenty-two passengers and fourteen crew under Captain Isaac Willett, including stewardess Mary Bourgogne, cabin boy George Ames, and Captain Willett's twelve-year-old son, John.

Only six of the passengers had purchased their tickets in advance for the late fall passage from New York to Portland. The remaining men, described as "poorly clad" and "in straitened circumstances," boarded as the ship was preparing to leave. Captain Willett recalled writing their names on a piece of paper so the stewardess could arrange for their cabins. *Chesapeake*'s Second Mate, Daniel Henderson, recognized Brain

*The Steamship Chesapeake*, by Eric Heyl. (USNHC)

from a trip two weeks earlier, when he had been accompanied by his "wife and child." This time, Brain introduced himself as the representative of an English steamship company and was sufficiently convincing that he was given a complimentary passage. According to a New York paper, the men boarded the vessel in separate parties, one group carrying four heavy trunks. The *Chesapeake* left New York on December 5. Ignoring each other, Brain and his men spent the next few days examining the vessel, quizzing the crew about their numbers, duties and stations on board and asking the firemen too many questions.

## *Capture Accomplished*

By the early hours of Monday, December 7, 1863, the *Chesapeake* was steaming about twenty miles north-northeast of Cape Cod. An icy wind froze the spray to the deck as the conspirators took their places. Captain Willett slept below while Second Engineer Odin Shaffer stood watch. Some time between one and two o'clock four men armed with pistols suddenly rushed into the engine room, shooting so close to fireman Patrick Connor that he had burn marks on his neck from the muzzle flashes of the pistols. Hearing the gunfire, Shaffer rushed aft to investigate only to flee in a hail of bullets. At least one struck him, and Shaffer soon collapsed, apparently at the engine room door. Chief Mate Charles Johnson was drinking coffee in his cabin nearby when he heard shots from the engine room. As he peered in, at least three of the five captors in the engine room opened fired on him. Johnson beat a hasty retreat, intent on informing the captain, and met the chief engineer, James Johnson, at the spot where Shaffer's body lay on the deck, legs dangling down the hatchway. At that point three conspirators hiding in *Chesapeake*'s pilot house joined two from the engine room in pursuit of the second mate, firing blindly and wounding him in the right knee and left arm.

Meanwhile, awakened by the chief mate, Captain Willett had stepped out of his cabin as the first of at least nine shots whistled past him: like his other officers, Willett was fortunate that the privateers were amateurs. Two more shots followed as he stooped to check on the lifeless Shaffer. Missed by several more shots, Willett finally came face to face with a pistol held by Lt. Parr, who declared him a prisoner of the Confederacy and handcuffed him. He was briefly confined to his cabin, then taken to the main cabin where the rest of the captives were held "in fear of their lives."

While all this transpired the chief engineer hurried to the engine room, the third of the steamer's officers to do so. What greeted James Johnson was not gunfire but a pistol against his head. Undeterred, Johnson grabbed the privateer's arm to prevent him from shooting, at which point another privateer, named Brooks, fired his pistol at the engineer who fled out the door. Johnson escaped, but with a bullet lodged firmly in his chin.

In the dark, the two Johnsons — the wounded mate and the engineer — scrambled into the kitchen and watched as Brain ordered three men to toss Shaffer's body over the side. Advised by the cook that the ship was taken, they reluctantly joined the rest of the captive passengers and crew in the main cabin. Using his medical skill, Parr later managed to remove a ball from the chief mate's arm but could not extract the one in his knee nor the one embedded in the engineer's chin.

Second Mate Daniel Henderson missed most of the action. He awoke only as four men broke through his cabin door and forced him to dress at gunpoint. They put him in irons, made him a prisoner of the Confederate States and locked him back in his cabin. Henderson managed to escape from his room, but slipped on the icy deck and was hauled into the pilot house where he spent the night. Although "not in the habit of being afraid under ordinary circumstances" he later admitted to being "in bodily fear" from the time of the capture until their release.

With the second engineer dead, the crew closely guarded and the captain in irons, *Chesapeake* was theirs. Only then did the captors suddenly realize that none of them — apparently not even George Robinson from St. Stephen who had enlisted in Brain's gang as the sailing master — knew how to navigate the vessel or maintain steam. The two engineers Brain had recruited in New York got so drunk the night before sailing he couldn't get them on board. Making do, he forced the injured engineer, James Johnson, to run the machinery and commandeered passenger Robert Osborne, a former New Brunswick ship captain, as the pilot.

Once this was all worked out, the *Chesapeake* set off for Grand Manan, New Brunswick, where Locke, with the letter of marque granted to the now-defunct Confederate privateer *Retribution,* was waiting. The ship arrived on December 8, and Brain and several of his men went ashore. Later a small pilot boat carried Locke and another man, who had joined the crew, out to the *Chesapeake*. With the crew complete and Locke, whom the Americans considered the real mastermind behind the scheme, aboard and the ship's original crew still under guard, *Chesapeake* headed for Saint John with the pilot boat in tow. During the day passengers and crew, except for the engine room personnel and the pilot, were transferred into the pilot boat. As they steered northwards, the captors painted over the ship's name and the distinctive yellow streak on her funnel. When *Chesapeake* was about three miles off Saint John, the pilot boat was cut loose and the captives allowed to row ashore. About four a.m. on the morning of December 9, Captain Willett and company raised the alarm in the sleeping city of Saint John.

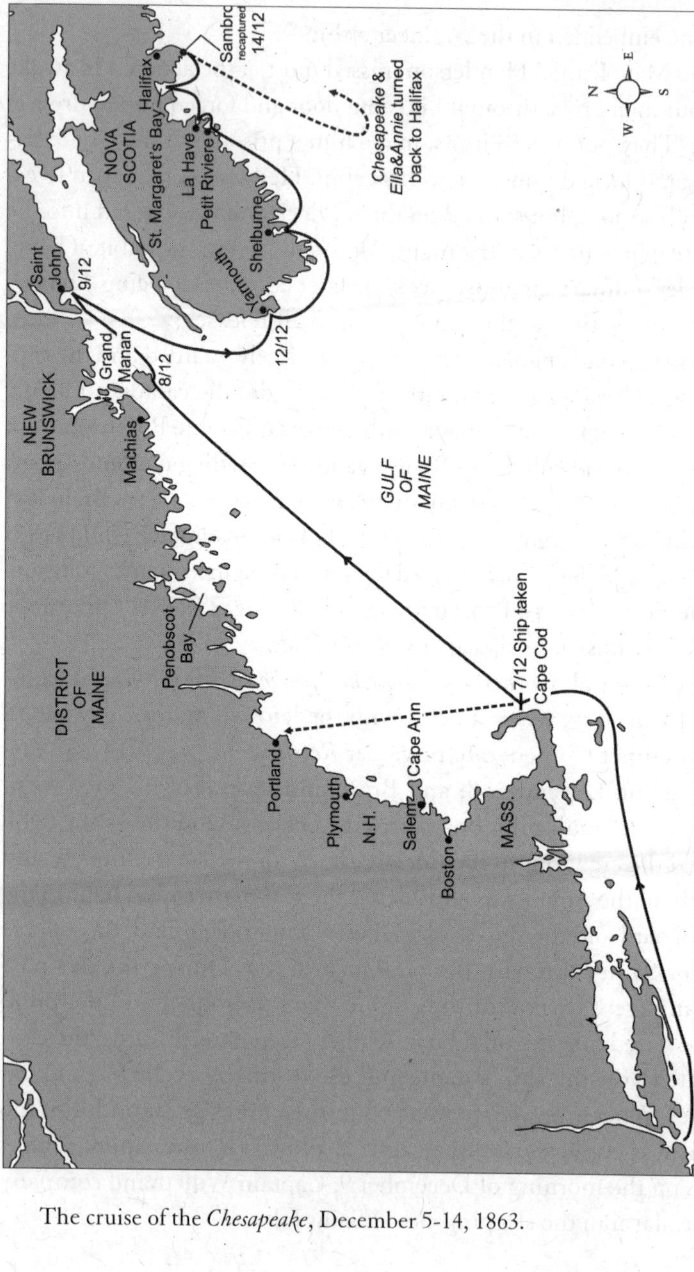


The cruise of the *Chesapeake*, December 5-14, 1863.

*Confederate Blockade Runner Ella & Annie,* by R.G. Skerrett. The only difference between the ship in this image and the USS *Ella & Annie* that recaptured the *Chesapeake* is the flag. (USNHC)

## *Recapture*

The new age of telegraphic communications made it hard for Brain and his gang of desperados to get very far before the news spread like wildfire. Within minutes of Willett's landing in Saint John, telegraph lines between local US consular offices and Washington began to hum. On behalf of the Union, James Howard, the consul in Saint John, sought warrants from the local magistrate to capture the *Chesapeake* "pirates" for their malicious, willful, felonious and piratical act. Meanwhile, gunboats from Boston, New York and Portland, delayed by heavy gales and ice, gradually began closing in on the freshly painted, newly christened *Retribution*.

Low on coal and supplies, the *Chesapeake* set off for Nova Scotia , where Brain hoped to secure both from the small settlements along the coast. Without funds of their own, except for the £87 passage money

Brain had seized from Captain Willett, the privateers soon began to sell off portions of the cargo to pay for fuel. This "breaking bulk" in a vessel that had not been legally condemned to the captors was a major offense under international prize law and usually resulted in the loss of the prize. It also entitled Her Majesty's Customs officials to confiscate whatever goods Brain had sold them from angry merchants and citizens.

At first, however, Brain and his band of privateers got a warm reception in Nova Scotia, as *Chesapeake* stopped in Yarmouth for coal on December 12, then La Have, Shelburne, Petite Rivière and St. Mary's Bay. News of the capture electrified the citizens of Halifax. "Southern daring has just added another feat to its list of astonishing achievements," proclaimed the *Halifax Morning Chronicle* on Thursday, December 10, 1863. Sometime before they reached Petite Rivière, Brain went ashore and headed to Halifax to raise more money and hire additional crew, leaving the so-called *Retribution* in the hands of Lt. Parr. It was in that tiny harbour near Lunenburg, that the privateers encountered the first of the Union hunters. What Parr saw was the large paddle steamer *Ella & Annie*, commanded by Lt. Nicholls, US Navy, freshly arrived from Boston. Parr may have recognized the steamer immediately, since the *Ella & Annie* had been a very famous Confederate blockade runner. For years she had outwitted and outrun Union forces, carrying cotton to export markets (with a payload of some 1441 bales she was seldom matched) and more precious cargo inbound. On December 9, 1863, however, the *Ella & Annie*'s luck ran out: she was captured at sea by the USS *Niphon* while carrying Austrian rifles, salt, beef, paper and saltpetre, as well as despatches for the Confederate government. When news of the capture of the *Chesapeake* reached Boston on December 10, the *Ella & Annie* was provisionally commissioned into the US Navy, and in a curious twist of fate, immediately despatched to hunt for the *Retribution*.

As the *Ella & Annie* approached Petite Rivière from the north, Parr slipped *Chesapeake* behind an island, and the hunter passed into Lunenburg without suspicion. Nicholls went ashore to use the local telegraph, and so did Parr — to warn Locke and Brain in Halifax. Only quick thinking by the local postmistress prevented the two protagonists from meeting. The American Vice-Consul in Nova Scotia later blamed the citizens of Petite Rivière for interfering with his attempt to capture Brain when the *Chesapeake* pulled in there, which says a great deal about local sympathies.

Finally, late in the day on December 13, at Sambro harbour, just fourteen miles from Halifax, Parr and the *Chesapeake* met up with the *Investigator* (Captain Holt), a small Halifax collier sent by Locke. On board the Nova Scotia vessel were the brothers William and Alexander Henry, engineers whom Locke had hired to replace the wounded Johnson. Brain and his gang now needed just one good day to refuel the *Chesapeake* and they could get to sea and on their way home. Unfortunately, early the next morning, just as the coaling was about to begin in the sheltered waters of Sambro harbour, the *Ella & Annie* steamed into view. The privateers abandoned their ships so quickly that they left behind their breakfast and the sleeping Henry brothers and privateer George Wade who were aboard the collier. Cleverly, one of the original *Chesapeake* crew who was still aboard raised the Union Jack upside down, the international signal of distress (although, given the nature of the Union Jack it was a rather dubious signal), and Lt. Nicholls seized the ship. He then searched Captain Holt's *Investigator* at gunpoint "in a very rough and tyrannical manner," seizing Wade, the Henry brothers and the luggage belonging to the hapless engineers. When Holt protested, Nicholls threatened to put him in irons like the others and take him to Boston as a "d . . . fine witness." Nicholls got a prize crew aboard the *Chesapeake,* and soon both it and the *Ella & Annie* were steaming their way to Portland, Maine.

Nicholls' rash act might well have been the beginning of a serious international incident but for the quick thinking of Captain A.G. Clary, USN, the captain of the USS *Dacotah.* By sheer chance Clary intercepted Nicholls en route and immediately realized the implications of a US naval vessel recapturing a Confederate prize in neutral waters. The *Ella & Annie*, *Chesapeake* and *Dacotah* altered course at once for Halifax, where Clary hoped to obtain British approval for the recapture.

In Halifax, the arrival of the *Chesapeake* escorted by two American warships and the accounts of her capture and recapture shocked the Maritimes. The engineer's murder was soundly condemned by the *Acadian Recorder* as a "cowardly act" and press criticism of the capture was harsh: "Although evidencing some skill in the planning [it] lacks the higher qualities of courage or heroism to extenuate it." The Saint John *Evening Globe* called the murder "simply infamous" and even the ordinarily pro-South *Express* condemned such "an act of arrant wickedness" committed by ruffians who shot one man, wounded two others and then ran off like "fools and dastards." The *Halifax Morning Chronicle* affirmed what most Maritimers probably felt about the whole affair: "it is certainly a subject of regret that life was sacrificed."

The American take on the whole thing, not surprisingly, was rather different. As the New York *Herald* noted, there did not appear to be any real Confederates involved: "The *Chesapeake* piracy, like every other crime against our commerce that has been committed under the cover of this war, was arranged on British soil and committed by British subjects. It does not appear that a Southerner was concerned in the seizure of the *Chesapeake*; but it was wholly done by a party of men of the kind known as Blue Noses — men with the cold blood and feeble circulation of reptiles." It is not clear what New Brunswickers felt, if anything, about the characterization of their Nova Scotia neighbours in such a way, but they may well have taken some satisfaction in knowing that Americans blamed someone else for the deed. American papers were also completely mistaken in the expectation that the vessel and crew would soon be handed over to American authorities and the conspirators would be swiftly dealt with.

## *Judgement*

The *Chesapeake* case centred on whether the capture of the ship and her cargo was a legitimate wartime act of a commissioned privateer against the property of an enemy, or an illegal act of piracy and murder on the high seas. Further, the whole affair was clouded by Lt. Nicholls' own act of piracy in Sambro harbour, not simply his removing the *Chesapeake* at gunpoint, but his armed search of the Halifax collier *Investigator* and his removal and detention of British subjects who were actually in British territory at the time. Given the lack of political rhetoric from either side, it seems that neither the American government nor the Confederacy really wanted anything to do with the decision. Lt. Nicholls' clumsy attempt to take both ship and hostages back to the United States embarrassed Lincoln's government and forced Secretary of State Seward to issue an immediate apology and promise of censure to Lord Lyons, the British ambassador in Washington. Lord Russell graciously accepted the apology on behalf of Her Majesty's government, and both considered the matter settled.

The Confederate government sent a commissioner, James B. Holcombe, to Halifax to investigate the case and, if necessary, secure the prize for the Confederacy. Holcombe concluded fairly quickly that "the expedition was devised, planned and organized in a British colony by Vernon G. Locke, a British subject, who . . . assumed to issue commissions in the Confederate service to British subjects on British soil without authority for so doing." Indeed, it was not even clear that Brain was a Confederate subject. In any event, Brain had divested himself "of the character of an officer engaged in legitimate warfare" by selling portions of the cargo before it was legally condemned as a prize. Not surprisingly, the Confederacy denied any involvement in the affair and recommended that it be "disclaimed and disproved."

While the Confederates washed their hands of the whole affair rather quickly, there was at least an expectation among Northerners that the men who took one of their vessels on the high seas, killed one officer and shot several others, and held both crew and passengers in captivity would be brought to justice. In this, the Americans were sadly disappointed.

In many ways the tone of the legal fallout from the *Chesapeake* affair was set on the day when the *Ella & Annie*, the *Chesapeake* and the USS *Dacotah* arrived in Halifax to seek permission to take lawful possession of the liner. Captain Clary had clearly made the right decision to return to Nova Scotia to try to redress Lt. Nicholls' indiscretion in Sambro harbour, but the Americans got a rough reception. In fact, when Nova Scotia Lieutenant-Governor Sir Arthur Hastings Doyle heard on Saturday December

19, that one of the American gunboats accompanying the *Chesapeake* into Halifax was holding three British subjects in irons aboard ship, he immediately told Captain Clary that none of the eight US warships by then in harbour could leave until the men were released.

Clary acted swiftly, but the Americans were met by an angry crowd as they landed their captives. A crowd of respectable — if not very sympathetic — Haligonians, including merchants, professionals, two members of the provincial government and the high sheriff as well as US Vice-Consul Gunnison assembled on Queen's Wharf for the handover of the Henry brothers from Halifax and George Wade from New Brunswick. The Henry brothers had, of course, done nothing illegal. But Gunnison was determined to arrest Wade as soon as the US Navy let him go. He had arranged for a police constable named Hutt to stand by on the wharf with a warrant. Others had different plans. Just as Wade's handcuffs were removed, a small boat rowed by two well-known oarsmen drew up to the wharf. Wade was hustled into the boat, and the men pulled rapidly away.

Policeman Hutt, his uniform covered by a drab overcoat and hat, shouted for the men to stop and drew his pistol. As the crowd urged the rowers on, Dr. William Almon grabbed Hutt's arm and stopped the policeman from shooting at Wade. Then Dr. Peleg Smith and Alexander Keith had to step in to prevent Hutt from shooting Almon. All three were arrested and charged with interfering with the police. John W. Ritchie, brother of New Brunswick Supreme Court Judge William Ritchie and Almon's brother-in-law and attorney, argued before the court that Dr. Almon had prevented bloodshed on the crowded wharf, a view shared by the mayor and an alderman. Despite evidence linking all three to clandestine pro-South activities, Almon (whose brother was in the Confederate intelligence service, the same organization that Brain allegedly worked for), Smith and Keith were released with a mild reprimand and Almon paid a light fine.

Wade quietly disappeared. And with the rest of the gang — Brain, Locke, Parr and the others — gone after their hasty abandonment of the *Chesapeake* in Sambro harbour, there was soon no one in Nova Scotia to hold accountable for the whole affair. It only remained to determine the disposition of the *Chesapeake* herself.

The case of who now owned the *Chesapeake* was heard by Alexander Stewart, CB, judge of the Nova Scotia Vice-Admiralty Court. This was the one court in the tangled skein of jurisprudence surrounding the *Chesapeake* affair that seemed to actually have jurisdiction over maritime law, and a place where the Americans might have expected justice. With eighteen years experience on the bench, Stewart was well respected but not well liked, and his odd behaviour during the trial of the *Chesapeake* did not add to his popularity. On Saturday, January 9, 1864, before a courtroom full of citizens and members of the local bar, Stewart announced his intention to hand the ship and its cargo over to the original owners as quickly as possible. He refused to admit a claim from either side. By breaking into and selling the cargo, the Confederate captors had forfeited their claim to the vessel. Then, in trying to recapture the *Chesapeake* in Canadian waters, Lt. Nicholls and Union naval vessels had committed such a grave breach of British neutrality, they too had lost all rights to the prize.

Lawyers for both parties were outraged, and many more were puzzled at hearing the verdict before the actual trial was held. The Halifax *Daily Evening Globe* supported Stewart as a "gentleman of independent integrity and qualifications as a lawyer," but the *Acadian Recorder* sympathized with the thousands of Nova Scotians who were deeply mortified by the judge's behaviour. They accused him of trying to serve as judge, jury and witness. The following day, Stewart tried to explain why he had gone ahead and presented his preliminary opinion that the case was in fact piracy, but the *Daily Evening Globe* was forced to admit that no two newspapers could agree on what the judge had meant and even the lawyers were confused.

The case rolled on and numerous witnesses were heard, but Stewart maintained his position. Finally, on February 15, 1864, he stated that although the seizure was undoubtedly piratical, there were many extenuating circumstances. He dismissed the US Navy case — that they lawfully recaptured the vessel — because the Nova Scotia Vice-Admiralty Court

Sir Arthur Hamilton Gordon, Lieutenant-Governor of the province (centre, with beard) at the time of the *Chesapeake* Affair, on the steps of Government House, Fredericton. (PANB)

had no prize jurisdiction between the United States and the Confederacy. Stewart's final decision restored the *Chesapeake* and cargo to the owners, subject to payment of expenses and security for future claims. The scale of court fees and expenses was high, including $1434.01 in costs incurred by the Nova Scotia Revenue Department and provincial government expenses of $2900. Although Judge Stewart gave up his fees in the case, the advocate general's fees were $270.75 and telegrams to and from Lord Lyons in Washington were $198.52.

As the Halifax Court of Vice-Admiralty gathered evidence in early January, Brain and three of his men — David Collins, Linus Seely and James McKinley — returned quietly to Saint John. They were soon arrested on warrants requested by US Consul Howard and signed by New Brunswick's lieutenant-governor, Arthur Hamilton Gordon. In the end, they were the only *Chesapeake* conspirators brought before the court for their actions.

The Court House, Saint John, ca. 1863. Both the original trial of the *Chesapeake* "privateers" and the appeal which freed them were held here. (NBM)

The warrants against Brain, Collins, Seely and McKinley sought extradition to the US under the Webster-Ashburton Treaty of 1842, the first such attempt to use the treaty to send alleged criminals across the border. According to Article 10 of the treaty, if a citizen of one nation sought asylum in another's territory for an act considered criminal in both places, such as "persons charged with the crime of murder, or assault to commit murder, or piracy or arson, or robbery or forgery, or the utterance of forged paper, committed within the jurisdiction of either of the high contracting parties," an appropriate judge could issue a warrant for extradition. And after examining the evidence of the captain and others, Lieutenant-Governor Gordon did not hesitate to issue a warrant for the local magistrate to proceed.

Apparently, Brain never actually appeared in court. Despite the reluctance of the Confederacy to accept Brain as an agent acting on their behalf, the Saint John courts did: he was simply cut loose. Meanwhile, local sympathy in Saint John was strongly in support of the other men, and that ultimately affected the outcome of the court cases.

The only formal trial of conspirators in the *Chesapeake* affair began on January 4, 1864, when Collins, Seely and McKinley appeared in Saint John Magistrate's Court before Justice Humphrey Gilbert. The three were accused of piracy and murder on the high seas within US jurisdiction. Counsel for the defence was none other than John Hamilton Gray, QC, former premier of the province, and later an expert on Canadian-American boundary issues. Gray was considered a brilliant orator and very skilful in the courtroom. He also had Confederate sympathies, and his brother had recently been killed on a Southern battlefield fighting for the rebel cause. In defence of the three men, Gray argued technicalities: firstly, that a magistrate's court lacked jurisdiction over piracy, and secondly, that by combining two separate crimes requiring different courts in one warrant, the warrant itself was bad. Unconvinced, Gilbert continued to hear the case, pronouncing his judgement on February 24, 1865. He not only found the three men guilty of piracy, but suggested that since the murder was committed on the deck of an American ship, it occurred within US jurisdiction and, therefore, constituted a rightful cause of extradition under the Webster-Ashburton Treaty.

Gray did not accept the judgement. He immediately demanded to see copies of the US Consul's request and other relevant documents. Preferring to cooperate rather than risk being subpoenaed as a witness, thereby forcing a disagreeable collision between the province's judicial and executive branches, Lt.-Gov. Gordon wisely decided to produce the documents. After reviewing the documents Gray applied for a writ of *habeas corpus*, and the case went before Sir William Johnstone Ritchie of the New Brunswick Supreme Court. A well-respected member of the New Brunswick bar, Ritchie — who happened to be the brother of Halifax barrister John W. Ritchie, who defended the prominent Halifax citizens who conspired in Wade's escape on the wharf — was noted for his probity and judgement.

After a number of weeks reviewing what he called a "novel, peculiar, delicate, but important case," on March 10, 1864 Judge Ritchie spent two hours explaining his findings to a packed courtroom. Basically he found that the prisoners had been illegally detained and that Saint John magistrate Humphrey Gilbert had no jurisdiction to deal with the case. Even if Judge Gilbert had jurisdiction, the warrant that Collins, Seely and McKinley were committed on was wrong and negated all subsequent actions. Further, Ritchie accepted Brain's orders from the Confederacy as legitimate and acquitted the accused because they were deemed to be belligerents. Nonetheless, Judge Ritchie concluded that an offense committed on the high seas could be tried in Nova Scotia and there was no need for the prisoners to be extradited. In the absence of proper charges, Ritchie ordered the men's release. He did recommend, however, that Collins, Seely and McKinley be charged under the *Foreign Enlistments Act,* and warrants were duly issued. But in the climate of the moment, the three men were local heroes and the order for re-arrest was never executed. Not surprisingly, American officials decried Saint John as a hot bed of Confederate sympathizers and denounced the judicial system as corrupt. As if to prove the point, shortly after the trial ended Collins's brother walked across the bridge between St. Stephen and Calais, Maine, and robbed a bank while brandishing a pistol and carrying a Confederate flag.

No one ever served time for any of the actions of Brain's gang of "privateers", no compensation or restitution was made to the United States, to Shaffer's family or to the men who were wounded. *Chesapeake* returned to her service as a liner, and the *Ella & Annie* was formally commissioned into the US Navy as the USS *Malvern* in February 1864 where she spent much of the rest of the war as the flagship of the North Atlantic Blockading Squadron.

## *Brain Strikes Again*

Brain and his crew soon headed over the snow-covered roads towards Lake Erie and the safety of a Confederate network used to guide escaping prisoners of war back to the South. Forced to flee empty-handed, Brain justified his capture of the *Chesapeake* by stating, "The affair has not cost the Confederacy a man or a cent and it has frightened the Yankees out of their senses."

The Old Saint John Court House, still in use today. (NBMHP)

When they reached Lake Erie, Brain and his men could not resist capturing a small lake steamer and running up the Confederate flag. They then spent a week plundering northern shipping on the lake before being forced to run the ship ashore and burn her to avoid capture. A story in the London, Ontario, *Free Press* of September 1864 described their "piratical raid" under the headline "The Steamer Island Queen Seized and Plundered." After a quick visit to his mother in Ohio near Lake Erie, Brain returned to navy headquarters at Richmond, Virginia, and his next assignment. But by then the south was virtually destroyed. "Colonel" Brain's naval career came to an end, not with surrender, but by sailing the last prize of the Confederacy into Kingston, Jamaica, and abandoning her to her fate: it seems that the New Brunswick courts may have been right about his Confederate status after all.

## Chapter Four

# The Legacy

By the time the *Chesapeake* cases were heard and the verdicts given, Brain was long gone from Atlantic Canada, and with him went the last of New Brunswick's pirates and privateers. As far as the local newspapers were concerned, the *Chesapeake* affair dwindled quickly from "astonishing" to "unpleasant" to "interminable." In New Brunswick, Judge William Ritchie's release of Brain's co-conspirators on a technicality conformed nicely with public sentiment. The release of Dr. Almon and his colleagues pacified public opinion in Halifax, and the return of the *Chesapeake* and cargo to the owners pleased both American and British mercantile interests. Almon went on to become the first dean of Dalhousie University Medical School, and Keith's family brewery business continues to this day. Their lawyer, the Hon. J.W. Ritchie, became Solicitor General of Nova Scotia.

As the excitement died down, Maritimers began to focus on their own political issues, among them some form of union that would allow the colonies to better protect themselves in the event of an American invasion following the end of the Civil War. The threat was real enough. Maritimers had rejected republicanism during the American Revolution, helping to beat back several attempts to draw them into the rebellion against Britain. Although the War of 1812 was never as serious a danger to the Atlantic colonies as it was to the Canadas, Nova Scotians, Newfoundlanders and New Brunswickers had not missed their chance to trim Yankee sails at sea while hostilities lasted between 1812 and 1814 — old ties of family, friendship and trade notwithstanding.

Sir William Ritchie, 1865. As Supreme Court Judge of New Brunswick, Ritchie threw out all the charges against the *Chesapeake* privateers in 1864. By 1868, he was the first chief justice of the Supreme Court of Canada. (NBM)

Sir John Hamilton Gray, former head of the provincial government, was the high-powered, smooth-talking Saint John lawyer who defended the *Chesapeake* privateers and won their appeal. He was later one of the Fathers of Confederation. (PANB P-37-43)

That latent dislike of Yankee republicanism loomed large in the *Chesapeake* affair of 1863-1864, both in the recruiting of "privateers" and the handling of the fallout in the courts. While many Canadians today empathize with the northern cause and focus on the participation of British North Americans in the Union army, the *Chesapeake* affair demonstrates the strength and depth of support for the Confederacy in what is now Atlantic Canada. Certainly, the northern press understood where Maritimer's sympathy lay, and it was no accident that they blamed British subjects for trimming a few more Yankee sails when they had the occasion.

It was no surprise, then, that during the US Civil War Maritimers sought to secure themselves against another round of potential American aggression. In fact, shortly after the *Chesapeake* affair, plans were formulated by Nova Scotia, Prince Edward Island and New Brunswick to meet in Charlottetown in the summer of 1864 to discuss a union. The colony of Canada, remote from the weight of British power and under even greater danger from the Americans, asked to participate, and the idea of an even larger union grew. That process, propelled by the massing of republican Irish veterans of the Union Army along the border and an attack into Upper Canada, eventually led in 1867 to the union of three colonies, Canada, Nova Scotia and New Brunswick, into the new Dominion of Canada. Border tensions and the aspirations of a few trimmers of Yankee ambition had a great deal to do with New Brunswick's involvement. Indeed, one of the Fathers of that Confederation was John Hamilton Gray, and the first chief justice of the Supreme Court of Canada was none other than William Ritchie.

## Acknowledgements

I would like to acknowledge the contribution of Professor Marc Milner in inciting, inspiring and improving this book. I am grateful to Jean Kitchen for editing a preliminary draft of the manuscript and to Robert Dallison for his assistance in tracking down illustrations and material from the New Brunswick Provincial Archives. Thanks are also due to my Dutch colleagues, Dr. Jaap de Moor and Professor Jaap Bruijn, for their ongoing interest in Canadian privateers. I would also like to thank Claudia Jew of The Mariner's Museum in Newport News, Virginia; Dayle Krause of the Queen's County Museum in Liverpool, Nova Scotia; Dan Conlin of the Maritime Museum of the Atlantic in Halifax, Nova Scotia; Lois Yorke of the Public Archives of Nova Scotia, and Jennifer Longdon from the New Brunswick Museum. It has been a delight working with Goose Lane Editions. I hope that readers will forgive any errors and enjoy the adventures of New Brunswick's privateers.

## Photo Credits

Photos and other illustrative material on the front cover and pages [10], 16 and 60 appear courtesy of the Bailey Collection, Mariner's Museum, Newport News, VA (MM); on pages 19, 21, and 45 courtesy of the National Archives of Canada (NAC); on pages 30-31, 35, 38, 82 and 87, courtesy of the Public Archives of New Brunswick (PANB); on page 51, courtesy of the Dalhousie University Archives and Special Collections, William Inglis Morse Collection (MS-6-7), Halifax NS (DUA); on page 43, the National Gallery of Canada (NGC); on page 57, courtesy of the Queen's County Museum, Liverpool, Nova Scotia (QCM); on pages 69, 83, 88, and on the back cover, courtesy of the New Brunswick Museum (NBM); on pages 71 and 75, courtesy of the United States Naval Historical Centre, Washington, DC (USNHC); and on pages 46 and 86, courtesy of the New Brunswick Military Heritage Project (NBMHP). The maps on pages 49, 52 and 74 are by Mike Bechthold. All illustrative material is reproduced by permission.

# Glossary

**Admiral** — The name admiral comes from the Arabic *amir* or *emir*, meaning prince. As the highest ranking officers in the Royal Navy, admirals commanded the fleet or one of its main divisions. Until 1864, admirals worked their way up through the blue, white and red squadrons from rear-admiral to vice-admiral and then to admiral, with the Admiral of the Red being the senior officer. The highest rank was Admiral of the Fleet.

**Admiralty** — The Admiralty was the British government department responsible for naval matters until 1964, when it became part of a unified Ministry of Defense. In the United States, the Department of the Navy is a branch of the Defense Department. Admiralty also means "sovereignty at sea," a concept administered by special maritime courts dealing with a wide range of civil and criminal matters including prizes seized by privateers and naval vessels.

**Ballast** — Vessels often carried heavy material such as beach rocks or iron as ballast in their holds to provide stability, with or without cargo. Ballast is a general term for any such material.

**Blockade** — Blockading required a number of naval vessels to patrol an enemy's coastline to ensure no shipping entered or left from the major ports. As a naval tactic, a blockade was designed to disrupt the movement of enemy warships and merchant vessels, reducing their ability to wage war by restricting the movement of their fleet, interfering with their supply routes and annoying the population by denying them food and trade essentials. Blockading was used with great success in both the War of 1812 and the Civil War. Those who sought to run ships in or out of blockaded ports were called blockade runners.

**Brig** — Brigs were small sailing vessels with two masts, both of which were rigged with square sails. Originally an abbreviation of brigantine, it eventually evolved into a distinct type of rig.

**Brigantine** — Brigantines were two-masted vessels with square sails on the foremast and triangular sails on the main mast. In the seventeenth century they were frequently used by pirates and were later favoured by navies for patrolling and communication.

**Broadside** — An extremely damaging battle tactic, the broadside involved simultaneously firing all the guns on one side of a ship of war at an enemy ship. It usually caused tremendous destruction and a huge loss of life.

**Buccaneers** — Lawless seamen who plundered ships in the Spanish main and the Pacific during the seventeenth century were called buccaneers, from the French word *boucan*, meaning smoke-dried beef and hides. The *boucaniers* who traded these goods later turned to attacking Spanish merchant ships. Since they did not attack ships of their own country, they were not considered pirates.

**Carronade** — Named after the Carron Iron Works in Scotland, carronades were developed in the late eighteenth century. These "smashers" were short-barrelled light guns that fired a heavy shot over a short distance and were extremely deadly in close fighting.

**Chebacco boat** — Named for the parish of Chebacco (now Essex) in Ipswich, Massachusetts, these small boats (rarely over forty feet long) with sharp sterns were developed as fishing schooners. Similar boats with square sterns were known as "dogbodies."

**Convoy** — A convoy is a group of merchant ships travelling together for mutual safety under the protection of one or more naval warships. Possibly developed as a defence against pirates, convoys were used during the Second World War to protect against submarine attack.

**Cruiser** — Naval cruisers were fast, well-armed frigates or sloops of war.

**Frigate** — Both the British and American navies built frigates in the early nineteenth century. They were fast three-masted warships with twenty to forty-four guns and only one complete gun deck.

**HMS** — His Majesty's Ship

**Letter of marque** — This letter or licence authorized a private vessel, whether a merchant ship or a cruising privateer, to seize an enemy ship and its cargo during wartime. The letter distinguished a privateer from a pirate and generally protected privateersmen from impressment. The term can refer to either the vessel or the authorizing letter itself.

**Marines** — Marines are soldiers who serve aboard ship or who work closely with naval forces. The first US Marine Corps was created in 1775, twenty years after the creation of a permanent marine force in Britain, known since 1924 as the Royal Marines.

**Privateer** — A privateer was either a privately owned vessel, heavily armed and crewed, with a government commission to sail against enemy shipping or a person who sailed in one. Privateers were an economical way to supplement a nation's naval power since they were outfitted, sailed and operated at the expense of the owners but under licence from the government. Also known as commerce raiding and *guerre de course*, privateering was abolished by the Treaty of Paris in 1856. The American refusal to sign the agreement meant that privateering became a feature of the Civil War of 1861-1865.

**Prize** — A prize was a captured enemy warship or merchant vessel and any cargo, later condemned by a Vice-Admiralty Court. The crew that sailed the prize to port was known as the prize crew under the command of a prize master.

**Prize Court** — Under international law or the Law of Nations, captured vessels had to be submitted to an authorized court (in Halifax, the Vice-Admiralty Court) where a judge reviewed documents and sworn affidavits from both parties and determined if the prize was "good and lawful." If so, it was condemned and the vessel and cargo became the property of the captor. If not, it was returned to the owners along with the various costs associated with capture.

**Prize money** — Prize money was the net proceeds the captors received from the process of bringing a captured vessel or cargo before a Vice-Admiralty Court and having it condemned.

**Schooner** — Probably derived from the Dutch word *schooner* or beautiful, schooners were common in America by the mid-1700s. They are sailing vessels with two or more masts set with fore-and-aft sails that can be sailed by a small crew.

**Sloop-of-war** — The navy sloop-of-war was a small three-masted full-rigged ship, with twelve to eighteen guns on a single deck, usually captained by a commander.

**Sloop** — Sloops are small vessels with a single mast and a mainsail with one or more jibs before the mast.

**Swivel** — Swivels were light, easily handled cannon mounted on a ship's railings around the upper deck or high on the mast so that they could be moved horizontally or vertically for aiming.

**USS** — United States Ship

**USRC** — United States Revenue Cutter

# Selected Bibliography


Cram, W. Bartlett. *Picture History of New England Passenger Vessels.* Hampden Highlands, ME: Burntcoat Corporation, 1980.

Bruce, Anthony and William Cogar. *An Encyclopedia of Naval History.* New York: Facts on File, 1998.

Caffrey, Kate. *The Lion and the Union: The Anglo-American War,* 1812-1815. London: André Deutsch, 1978.

Chappelle, Howard. *The History of American Sailing Ships.* 1935, rpt. New York: Bonanza Books, 1982.

Garritee, Jerome R. *The Republic's Private Navy: The American Privateering Business as Practised by Baltimore during the War of 1812.* Middletown, CN: Wesleyan University Press, 1977.

Graham, Gerald S. *Empire of the North Atlantic: The Maritime Struggle for North America.* Toronto: University of Toronto Press, 1958.

Gwyn, Julian. *Frigates and Foremasts. The North American Squadron in Nova Scotia Waters, 1745-1815.* Vancouver: University of British Columbia Press, 2003.

Hay, David and Joan. *The Last of the Confederate Privateers.* New York: Crescent Books, 1977.

Heidler, David S. and Jeanne T., eds. *Encyclopedia of the War of 1812.* Santa Barbara, CA: ABC-Clio, 2004.

Hickey, Donald. *The War of 1812: A Forgotten Conflict.* Urbana, IL: University of Illinois Press, 1989.

Kilby, William Henry. *Eastport and Passamaquoddy: A Collection of Historical and Biographical Sketches.* Eastport, ME: Ed. E. Shead, 1988.

Leefe, John. *The Atlantic Privateers: Their Story — 1749-1815.* Halifax: Pentheric Press, 1978.

Lydon, James. *Pirates, Privateers and Profits.* Upper Saddle River, NJ: Gregg Press, 1970.

Marquardt, Karl Heinz. *The Global Schooner: Origins, Development, Design and Construction, 1695-1845*. London: Conway Maritime, 2003.

Marquis, Greg. *In Armageddon's Shadow: The Civil War and Canada's Maritime Provinces.* Montreal: McGill-Queen's University Press, 1998.

Macnutt, W.S. *New Brunswick, A History: 1784-1867*. Toronto: Macmillan Canada, 1963.

Mcintosh, Dave. *The Collectors: A History of Canadian Customs and Excise.* Toronto: N.C. Press, 1984.

Padfield, Peter. *Maritime Power and the Struggle for Freedom: Naval Campaigns that Shaped the Modern World, 1788-1851.* London: John Murray, 2003.

Robinson, William Morrrison, Jr. *The Confederate Privateers.* 1928, rpt. Columbia: University of South Carolina Press, 1990.

Snider, C.H.J. *Under the Red Jack*. Toronto: Musson, 1927.

Stivers, Reuben Elmore. *Privateers & Volunteers. The Men and Women of Our Reserve Naval Forces 1766 to 1866*. Annapolis, MD: Naval Institute Press, 1975.

Stockton, Alfred. *Reports of Cases Decided in the Vice-Admiralty Court of New Brunswick from 1879-1891*. Saint John: J. & A. McMillan, 1894.

Winks, Robin W. *The Civil War Years, Canada and the United States.* 1960 rpt. Montreal: McGill-Queen's University Press, 1998.

# Index

**D**



**E**



**F**

## S



## T



## U

## The New Brunswick Military Heritage Project

The New Brunswick Military Heritage Project, a non-profit organization devoted to public awareness of the remarkable military heritage of the province, is an initiative of the Brigadier Milton F. Gregg, VC, Centre for the Study of War and Society of the University of New Brunswick. The organization consists of museum professionals, teachers, university professors, graduate students, active and retired members of the Canadian Forces, and other historians. We welcome public involvement. People who have ideas for books or information for our database can contact us through our website: www.unb.ca/nbmhp.

One of the main activities of the New Brunswick Military Heritage Project is the publication of the New Brunswick Military Heritage Series with Goose Lane Editions. This series of books is under the direction of Marc Milner, Director of the Gregg Centre, and J. Brent Wilson, Publications Director of the Gregg Centre at the University of New Brunswick. Publication of the series is supported by a grant from the Canadian War Museum.

THE GREGG CENTRE FOR THE STUDY OF WAR & SOCIETY UNIVERSITY OF NEW BRUNSWICK

Canadian War Museum Musée canadien de la guerre

## The New Brunswick Military Heritage Series

**Volume 1**

*Saint John Fortifications, 1630-1956,*
Roger Sarty and Doug Knight

**Volume 2**

*Hope Restored: The American Revolution and the Founding of New Brunswick*, Robert L. Dallison

**Volume 3**

*The Siege of Fort Beauséjour, 1755*, Chris M. Hand

**Volume 4**

*Riding into War: The Memoir of a Horse Transport Driver, 1916-1919*, James Robert Johnston

**Volume 5**

*The Road to Canada: The Grand Communications Route from Saint John to Quebec*, W.E. (Gary) Campbell

**Volume 6**

*Trimming Yankee Sails: Pirates and Privateers of New Brunswick*, Faye Kert

**Volume 7**

*War on the Home Front: The Farm Diaries of Daniel MacMillan, 1914-1927*, edited by Bill Parenteau and Stephen Dutcher

**Volume 8**

*Turning Back the Fenians: New Brunswick's Last Colonial Campaign*, Robert L. Dallison

**Volume 9**

*D-Day to Carpiquet: The North Shore Regiment and the Liberation of Europe,* Marc Milner

**Volume 10**

*Hurricane Pilot: The Wartime Letters of Harry F. Gill, DFM, 1940-1943,* edited by Brent Wilson with Barbara J. Gill

**Volume 11**

*The Bitter Harvest of War: New Brunswick and the Conscription Crisis of 1917*, Andrew Theobald

**Volume 12**

*Captured Hearts: New Brunswick's War Brides,* Melynda Jarratt

**Volume 13**

*Bamboo Cage: The P.O.W. Diary of Flight Lieutenant Robert Wyse, 1942-1943*, edited by Jonathan F. Vance

## About the Author

Privateers and pirates hunting their prey out of Atlantic Canadian ports have been Faye Kert's passion for many years. In 1997, she received her PhD from the University of Leiden, The Netherlands. Scholars consider her thesis, published as *Prize and Prejudice: Privateering and Naval Prize in Atlantic Canada in the War of 1812*, to be the authoritative text on the topic.

Kert has worked on two important underwater archaeological projects: the discovery, survey, and excavation of a 16th-century Basque whaling vessel at Red Bay, Labrador, and the raising of Henry VIII's flagship *Mary Rose* in Portsmouth, England. She is a member of the Canadian Nautical Research Society and the book review editor of the association's journal, *The Northern Mariner*. A former federal civil servant, Kert is a popular speaker before audiences ranging from cruise-ship passengers to professional historians.